Living in harmony
with your puppy

By Nicole Mackie

Foreword by Turid Rugaas

ISBN: 978-0-9554253-0-1
RRP: £9.95 ($US18.95)

First published in the United Kingdom in 2008
Paperclip Publishing, Stoke-on-Trent, UK
Editing and layout design: Liz Peters
liz.peters@ntlworld.com

Second Edition © 2011
Printed and bound by Lulu.com

Photographs by:

Nicole Mackie, Lyndsay Wilson, Mary Eggers, Ray and Jo Haddon, Lynne Cooper and Gail Dodd	(Labrador retrievers);
Claire Hart and Gael Stenton	(Lagotto romagnolos);
Shirley Coxon and Margaret Davies	(Bernese mountain dogs):
Shirley Coxon	(Havanese);
Lyndsay Wilson	(Jack Russell terrier);
Anne-Lill Kvam	(Shiba inu);
Kevin Kelly and Johann de Lange	(Lhasa apso);
Hilary Boxer and Sue Martin	(Bedlington terrier);
Nora Deaville	(Patterdale/Staffordshire cross);
Chris Griffiths	(Basset hounds and dachshunds);
Lynne O'Reilly	(Newfoundlands);
Mandy Worby	(Dalmatians);
Jane Baker	(Parson Russell terriers);
Melanie Bunker	(Golden retriever);
Kristy Mackie	(Australian terrier);
Carol Ilic	(Border collies).

Dedication

I would like to dedicate this book to Jesus Christ who taught us to value all animals, and to my husband Ian and my mother Elezabeth. All have been an inspiration and support to me while writing. Thank you.

Bible scripture

"But ask the animals and they will teach you, the birds of the air and they will tell you. Or speak to the earth and it shall teach you: and the fishes of the sea and they shall declare to you. Who does not know in all these that the hand of the Lord has done this? In whose hand is the soul of every living thing, and the breath of all mankind."
- Job 12v7-10

Thanks

I would like to give a special thanks to Sheila Harper for her mentorship in passing on her knowledge and understanding of canine behaviour; and to Turid Rugaas for sharing her knowledge of canine calming signals and training techniques. Thanks also to Sally Askew for her influence in helping me to look more deeply at the link between health issues and behaviour.

Foreword

Dear reader,

You are so lucky! This little book will give you simple, clear and understandable information on how to give your new puppy a good start in life. It is so important to make the start a good and friendly one to ensure mental and physical health for the dog. Follow the advice in this book and you may be able to avoid most of the problems that so often occur, mostly because we didn't think about it, or did the wrong things out of ignorance. This book can be a good guide for you, helping your puppy to become a happy dog, coping with life.

Enjoy the book, and I wish you good luck with your new puppy. Give him the good life he needs and deserves!

Turid Rugaas

Dog trainer, author and speaker

Norway

Preface

Growing up with dogs on New Zealand's Canterbury Plains was fun. Our first dog was a beagle, followed by a corgi and then a chihuahua. Years later when my own children were growing up, we purchased our own family dog, this time a pedigree Labrador retriever we named Olly.

Like most new puppy owners with older children we thought we were doing the right thing. After all, we were not new to dogs and did everything the books said to do. Unfortunately Olly suffered because of our lack of knowledge. He became hyperactive, over the top and quite hard to handle. We took him to dog obedience classes, ring craft classes, agility classes and for long daily walks as the books told us to do, but the more we did with him, the worse his behaviour became.

Sadly at the young age of two years, Olly died of a malignant tumour. Could this have been the consequence of long-term stress? We will never know but the possibility stays in our minds.

By the time Olly died we had purchased another Labrador we named Bella. We knew from Bella's two months in a depressed state after Olly died that dogs also feel grief when a member of their family dies.

Not wanting to put Bella in the same situations as Olly, I began to learn more about dog behaviour. I started working as a veterinary nurse in our local veterinary practice. We moved to Auckland where I studied general animal science and veterinary nursing. As a dog breeder at the time with my new qualification, I still felt dogs were highly misunderstood - there was still much more to learn.

I phoned a local dog training franchise and was taught their techniques of using check chains, water pistols and throw chains as aversive action to stop unwanted behaviour. I was told that check chains didn't hurt the dog; but if you place a check chain around your own upper arm and give it a tug ... it hurts! I did not know this at the time.

The check chains appeared to work for a short time but I had about four Labrador retrievers and a Siberian husky by this stage and one Labrador in particular was very sensitive. The check chains and throw chains only caused her to withdraw and shut down. Instead of building a good relationship with her, our relationship was damaged and it took some time to rebuild her trust.

When using the check chains on Bella, she became fearful and defensive of other dogs. For example: when we saw another dog and she wanted to rush to it, only to play, I would give a tug on the check chain as commonly taught in many books and training centres, so that she would realise she could not go and play unless I said she could. However, the tug on the check chain gave her the association that the other dog had caused the pain on her neck and therefore the other dog was something to be concerned about.

Every time she was tugged on the check chain for looking, lungeing or pulling to get to another dog, was yet another opportunity for her to make the association that other dogs were not nice and something to be afraid of. This was a completely different association to the one I thought she was learning. Dogs learn by association, but not always the association we think they are learning. As a result Bella became defensive about other dogs. In her case the check chain had damaged her relationships with other dogs.

After moving to the UK, I started using a clicker and soon became a clicker trainer with success. This was working well on some of my dogs and it was a non-adversory method (so I thought). However, one of my dogs was sound-sensitive. Each time I got the clicker out, she would start to pant and froth at the mouth, her stress levels would rise, she could not think and as a result could not be trained very well. I found that many dogs were sound-sensitive and did not like the clicker (even when using the latest soft-sounding clickers). Should we force these dogs to learn by the clicker or find a better way for the sensitive ones?

I realised from my dog's behaviour that I still needed to learn more, so went on to spend many years studying canine psychology, canine behaviour and training techniques. All gave me a good toolbox of knowledge and skills but I still had not found the answers needed to help my dogs and others with the same problems.

When I met Sheila Harper, she introduced me to a new concept of understanding dogs. She was my mentor for four years as I attended her International Dog Behaviour and Training School and worked with her, helping out with training classes and seminars. I have Sheila to thank for opening my eyes to a deeper understanding of canine behaviour, body language and how health, nutrition, environment and so much more relate to our dogs' behaviour.

During my time with Sheila I was introduced to other well-known speakers, such as Turid Rugaas, Anne-Lill Kvam, Sally Askew and many more; all who have added to my current repertoire of experience and knowledge of dogs.

I now live with three happy Labrador retrievers and experience a good relationship of trust and understanding with each dog. I cannot say I have made it and have all the answers, but I continue to learn from my dogs and continue to study and develop my skills.

I have written this book in order to help new puppy owners in the hope that they will not make the same mistakes I have made with my dogs, but will learn from the knowledge in this book how to observe and gain a better understanding of their dogs' needs, behaviour and body language. I hope owners can then fully enjoy living with their puppy.

Contents

Introduction

Your puppy is a precious gift to you. A friend who will share numerous adventures, joys and memories for many years to come. As your puppy's new parent, it is your responsibility to care for the needs of this precious gift throughout its life.

Your puppy has needs that are both physical and emotional, similar to the needs of humans. Meeting the needs of your puppy works like a feedback system - when you love and respect your puppy he will be willing to love and respect you in return.

It is very important that your puppy gets a good start in life and that owners learn how puppies communicate their needs. Only then will you be able to observe and understand his body language, calming signals, health and nutritional needs.

Its not always easy to know which breed best suits you or how to find a good breeder, but it is important you do a little research beforehand so that you have no regrets.

Chapter one

Finding the right breed

When searching for the breed that most suits your lifestyle, it is wise to do a little research beforehand, to find out about any breeds that may be appealing and which breed types may suit your home environment and lifestyle.

Puppies come in many different shapes, sizes, colours and breeds and require different levels of health care, maintenance and emotional support. Some of their needs can be attributed to the genetic make-up of the breed, while others can be a direct result of dietary or lifestyle influences.

Every puppy is born with instinctive behaviour patterns. Although these instincts are present in all breeds of dog, some breeds are purposefully bred for more strongly imprinted specific behaviour. Such behaviour can be triggered more easily if the puppy is bred to maximise it, then given the opportunity or environment to fully develop that behaviour.

For example, my first Labrador would run around and chase a ball with our children in the back yard quite frequently. The children loved the games and so did the dog. However, we did not realise at the time that we were strengthening his chase behaviour every time we played this game. The outcome of the games meant that our dog would chase anything that moved when out on a walk. He would chase joggers, cyclists, other families playing games in the park and other dogs. The instinct became so strong it was almost impossible to stop it without a long-term behaviour modification programme. We did not fully understand what we were really teaching our dog by allowing the chase games to continue. We learned the hard way how strong instinctive behaviour can be.

Speak to a veterinarian or a variety of breeders, including the kennel club, or to specialist breed clubs about the development and possible health issues to be aware of for your favoured breeds. It may help to give you a better understanding of the breeds and whether or not the breed you favour would really be the best choice for you.

Do your research first and find out all you can, before you choose your breed.

Check list for choosing a breed

The following is a list of questions to consider before choosing the breed of puppy that is best for you:

- How much time and attention will the puppy need and how much time and attention are you prepared to give?
- How much exercise will it need during development and how much exercise will it need once it is fully grown?
- How much fur grooming, nail trimming and visits to professional groomers will it need and what will this cost? Breeds that do not shed their coats require regular grooming and trimming.
- Does the breed shed its coat? You may not want a house full of hair when the grown puppy sheds its coat, sometimes twice a year - hair can get everywhere. Some breeds shed profusely once or twice a year, while others shed all year round.
- What is its life expectancy? Most larger breeds have a shorter life expectancy than smaller breeds.
- What type of bite should it have (over bite, under bite or scissor bite), what bite is best for the health of dogs?
- Should it have a black nose or a pink nose (pink-nosed

dogs can be susceptible to sunburn)?

- Are there any dietary requirements for this particular breed? Is it susceptible to food allergies or intolerances?
- What health issues is the breed susceptible to (eye problems, digestive problems, skin problems, hip or elbow dysplasia, etc)?
- Perhaps a crossbreed or rescue is a choice worth considering for you, rather than a purebred puppy with a pedigree. After all, there are many unwanted dogs in rescue centres waiting for loving people to adopt them.

Male versus female

In my own years of experience as a breeder, I have found that every litter is different and each individual puppy is different to its litter mates. It may not bother you whether you have a male or female unless you are planning to breed, as long as the puppy is happy and healthy. There are a few points to consider before you decide which gender of puppy you want. The list is as follows:

Female

- It is unusual for a purebred female puppy to grow larger than her mother, so look at the mother and you will get an idea of the size your female puppy may be as an adult.
- In general the females of the litter will be slightly smaller than the males.
- If you choose to spay your puppy she will have to undergo invasive surgery under anaesthetic. Many stitches, internal and external, are involved. There is always risk involved in any surgery but it will prevent unwanted puppies.
- If the female is not spayed, she will come into season once or twice a year, depending on the breed.
- When in season, this will last approximately three weeks and may attract males to the property, or she may try to look for males.
- If not spayed, her oestrus cycle may affect her temperament at specific times of the year. She may become more moody,

3

depressed, or more hyperactive.
- Intact females are more likely to develop mammary tumours.

Male
- Males are most likely to grow slightly larger than their female litter mates. Look at the size of the father and you will get an indication of the size your male puppy may become as an adult.
- Males can get surges of the hormone testosterone which can cause mounting behaviour. This can develop into an embarrassing problem if not dealt with correctly.
- Males can sometimes have a problem with one or both undescended testicles. Such dogs can never be used as stud dogs.
- If you choose to castrate your male puppy he will go under anaesthetic and surgery with just a few stitches to rejoin the skin.
- After castration there is a reduction in the hormone testosterone, making him less interested in a female in season, but he will need to be kept away from females in season for some time if he has been displaying mounting behaviour.
- Castration can change the male's temperament a little but this depends on the dog - in many cases there is little noticeable change in the dog's temperament.
- Castration may cure a humping problem if the issue is hormonal. If not, then other health or lifestyle issues may need to be considered.
- An intact male can scent a female in season up to five kilometres away. He may try to find a way to get to her.
- It is now possible for owners who want 'their boy' to retain his intact illusion to have implants (neutricals) inserted at the time of castration.

Chapter two

Finding the right breeder

Once a decision has been made as to the breed and gender of your new puppy, the next step is to find a good, reputable breeder whether your puppy is to be purebred or a crossbreed. Gain as much information as possible on the breed you have chosen. If you are looking at a crossbreed you may need to research two or more different breeds depending on how much cross breeding is involved.

The Kennel Club can also provide you with a list of rescue centres or breeders to contact. But be aware that not all who register their puppies, who show dogs, who own champions or even those that

judge, handle or train dogs, are necessarily reputable breeders.

You will need to ask the breeder questions, visit the breeder's home and view the living conditions of the dogs.

The breeder you have chosen to purchase a puppy from should be open, honest and approachable, should welcome visitors to see how the dogs live and should be able to provide you with copies of all the appropriate paperwork and health checks.

It is worth speaking to your veterinarian, who may be able to recommend good breeders or give you some information on the breeds you have chosen.

Check list for finding the right breeder

- Make sure you view the parents of the puppies and observe how they react to you.
- Try to walk outdoors with the parents if the breeder will let you, to see how they react with other dogs and people.
- Do the puppies and parents look happy, clean and healthy?
- Are the parents cowering, or running away from you or barking uncontrollably? This could indicate temperament problems which could be passed on to the puppies.
- Is their housing clean and fresh, with fresh bedding and clean water?
- Is the mother still with the puppies? The mother should be with the puppies until she has finished her job of feeding and teaching them. This could take 10 weeks or more.
- Ask if you will have a choice or if the breeder will choose the puppy for you.
- Ask what type of socialisation the breeder will do with the puppies before they go to new homes.
- Is the puppy raised in the home around people or isolated, away from human contact?
- Ask what health clearances the parents have and view all paperwork.
- Do you like what you see? If you don't like what you see then say thank you and politely leave.
- When you do find a good breeder, be prepared to be

6

questioned and even have your home checked out by the breeder. A good breeder will want to know where the puppy is going to live.

What comes with the package?

The breeder should provide you with more than just a puppy. You should have copies of all necessary documents, such as x-ray results, eye certificates of the parents or any other clearances required for your particular breed.

You will most likely be given a diet sheet to say what is being fed to your puppy and how many times a day and any special dietary needs of your puppy.

Your breeder should want to keep in close contact with you and give advice at any time throughout the puppy's life.

If you ever need to re-home the puppy at any time in its life, the breeder should be prepared to take it back or help you re-home it, no matter what the age.

Your breeder should give you a puppy pack similar to the above, containing as much information as possible on your puppy, a sample of the food it has been eating, inoculation certificates, pedigree chart, health status of both parents and any important information on the care and health of your puppy.

7

Your puppy should be taken to your veterinarian within 48 hours of purchase. Most breeders will recommend this. Your breeder should be only too happy to do anything possible to help you if required at any stage of your puppy's life.

These puppies are living in a clean, fresh nursing area.

Choosing your puppy

Through conversation with you, your breeder should have a good understanding of what you are looking for in a puppy and should also know the different temperaments within the litter, so is sometimes the best person to pair you with the right puppy.

Your breeder may have already chosen a specific puppy from the litter for you (many breeders do not allow you to choose). If the breeder allows you to choose your puppy, then refer to the *check list for choosing your breed* on page two.

Look at what type of socialisation the puppy has been exposed to - has the puppy met children of a variety of ages and people of different life stages? Has he been in a car? Has he been with his mother long enough for her to teach him the life skills he needs to learn before leaving her at around 10 weeks of age or older, depending on the mother. Some mothers may take around 10 weeks to complete weaning and training such as bite inhibition, or some may take longer. It is very common for puppies to go to new homes at around eight weeks of age but they will settle into their new homes more quickly if they are with their mother a little longer and this will also help to avoid many problems later on.

If your breeder is planning to let her puppies go at just eight weeks old or less, ask her if she will keep your puppy with its mother for another week or two. Some breeders will be happy to do this. If she is not prepared to keep the puppy with its mother, then it may be in the best interest of your puppy to take it when the breeder is prepared to let it go.

My own Siberian husky was an excellent mother and did not finish weaning or teaching her puppies until they were 12 weeks of age. In my years of experience with many dogs and puppies, I have found that they can be successfully socialised for many months, right into adulthood.

Another of my Labrador retrievers did not begin her socialisation programme until she was 13 months old. Two months into the programme she was beginning to help other dogs with socialisation skills and ever since, has been helping many dogs with fear and other social difficulties with dogs. All these issues are important to the puppy's development. A good foundation will help him cope with the challenges of life.

Your puppy's future

Deciding on a puppy's future before it has had time to develop its own personality, confidence, abilities, coping skills and relationship with its owner may be setting up both owner and puppy for possible disappointment. Not all puppies will grow to develop the skills we may wish them to develop. It is best to wait and give the puppy time. If the skills do not develop the way we hoped, does it really matter? Are we not better off with a happy, healthy puppy?

One of my own dogs loves to meet weekly with her friends and

Social walk group in the forest. This is how many dogs can learn correct socialisation and life skills.

walk in the forest with them. However, another of my dogs cannot cope with meeting other dogs in the forest. To make her walk with other dogs causes her too much stress. To place her in this situation is neither kind nor helpful to her and would only increase her problem. Your puppy will develop his own individual character. He will be able to make choices and if given the opportunity in life will develop his own talents, enjoyment, relationships, likes and dislikes, just as we humans do.

Your puppy will need to know he can trust you and that he is loved and respected. We can do this in many ways by calm interactive games with our puppy such as nose-work, sitting while massaging, or gently stroking and talking softly to your puppy. These calm interactions will help your relationship with your puppy to develop more than any high-activity exercise games.

Perhaps one of the best things we can do for our puppy is to learn canine language, also known as calming signals. It is then that we can really understand what our puppy is telling us, what he needs and whether or not he likes or dislikes something, or if what

The Labrador puppies below are investigating and learning about the garden. Tails high and paw lift indicate high arousal along with a little fear.

This Jack Russell terrier puppy is happy exploring the outdoor faucet.

we think he likes may be caused by other issues in the puppy's life, such as health, obsession, stress or over-excitement.

Become an observer of your puppy. The skills of learning your puppy's calming signals won't come naturally but the more you observe your puppy and other dogs you come in contact with, the more skilled you will become.

Preparing for your puppy's arrival

Now you have chosen your breed and a breeder, you will have a little time now to prepare for your puppy's arrival. There will be many things to think about such as which equipment to use on your puppy - collar or harness, length of lead, diet, bedding and whether your house and yard are safe and secure areas for your puppy. You may want to check that both your house and your garden are puppy-proof. There are many poisonous plants that grow in most countries. For a list of poisonous plants, you can refer to your country's national poisons register, or check the internet.

It is not just poisonous plants that could harm your puppy. There are also many things around the home that could place your puppy in danger such as the contents of rubbish bins, electric wires or cables, phones, computers, glassware or china and children's toys.

Make sure there are no toxic plants in the garden that your puppy could chew.

Even some food items can be dangerous if swallowed, such as large pieces of bone, cooked bones (from which sharp brittle pieces can break off), avocado stones, corn cobs and many more.

Look around your home and if it is not toddler-proof, then it probably is not puppy-proof either. It is much easier to place things out of reach than to put your puppy at risk. This is only temporary. Once your puppy has learned the house rules, finished teething and passed puppyhood and adolescence you should be able to place things back to normal again. Below is a check list of a few basic items you may need and things to do before the arrival of your puppy:

- Check that your house and yard are puppy-proof
- Flat, wide, soft collar for a name tag

11

Your puppy may just want to sit in the garden and sniff the flowers.

- Flat, soft, well-fitting harness
- Name and address tag - required by law in some countries, but a safety precaution wherever you live
- Long walking lead - should be at least two metres in length
- Soft brush for grooming
- Food bowl - stainless steel
- Water bowl, preferably stainless steel. Water must be available at all times
- Food - daily quantity will depend on the dog
- Bed, basket or crate for puppy to sleep in
- Warm, dry, comfortable bedding
- Toys, preferably soft ones at this stage
- Kong - to stuff with tasty food and help the puppy to settle
- Nail clippers
- Soft towels to dry the puppy on rainy days or after a bath
- Toothbrush (if you plan to clean your puppy's teeth yourself)
- Pick-up bags (for you know what)

Bringing home the puppy

This is when life really gets exciting ... the day you bring home your new baby puppy. However, to make this a little easier for your puppy, try to arrange with your breeder to allow you to visit him a couple of times before you finally collect him so that he already knows and trusts you.

A few days before you collect him, give your breeder a small cloth or towel which can be placed with the mother and other siblings. You can take it home with the puppy as it will contain their smell for a number of days and help with the settling-in process for the puppy.

Allow the puppy to have this cloth as much as he likes and to sleep with it. It may be dirty and smelly but to your puppy it will be a comfort and you can throw it away or wash it after a few days when he is more settled.

When you collect your puppy, try to have another person with you who can sit in the back of your car with the puppy, especially if you have a long distance to cover. Stop a few times in safe places to allow the puppy to relieve himself and drink some water if he

Have someone sit with your puppy on the journey home.

needs to. Your puppy may be a little worried and cry or bark, especially if this is his first time in a car or away from his mother and siblings.

He may or may not settle on the journey, so try to be patient with him, after all, this will be a very traumatic time for him. A few drops of rescue remedy (Bach flowers) or other calming herbal remedies may help the puppy to stay more calm during travelling.

Exploring his new home

Once you get your puppy home, take him out into your garden area immediately so he can relieve himself. Allow him to walk around and explore the area - he will need to check things out.

Open the door into your house and allow him to go in when he

After exploring outdoors your puppy will want to investigate indoors.

is ready and check that out too. Speak softly to him and walk very slowly with him so you do not frighten him with quick movements. Show your puppy where his bed is and where his water and toys are. Puppies feel grief when taken from their mum and siblings. Getting over this grief period will take time and a little understanding from you.

The needs and demands for your puppy will be great for his first few weeks while he settles into his new home and family. He will need a lot of time, patience and understanding as he learns and explores the rules and routines of his new family.

Try not to leave the puppy alone during the first few weeks to give him adjustment time and time to bond with you. If you need to go out for a length of time, take the puppy with you if it is safe to do so, or have someone else stay with your puppy for the time you are away.

Leaving a puppy alone is similar to leaving a small child alone. They can become very frightened as they do not understand why they are alone or where their trusted owner has gone. A puppy left alone may develop many problems such as barking, inability to rest, hyperactivity, destructive behaviour, shadow chasing, chewing everything and many more problems and health issues. This is even worse if the puppy is left alone outdoors.

If you need to work a few hours a day try to have someone care for your puppy or at least be there to let the puppy outdoors once or twice to relieve himself and perhaps sit calmly with him for a few minutes.

If neither of these options is possible then try to build up your puppy's time alone little-by-little before he is left alone in the house.

This can be done by starting with leaving him alone for just a few seconds a few times a day in the room he will be left in when you are away.

After a few days if he is coping well with this you could try leaving him for one or two minutes just two or three times a day. Do this for a few days and if the puppy is coping well, increase the time little-by-little until he can be safely left for the timespan needed. Do not rush his training. It may take many days or weeks for him to cope with being left alone. You may want to take some holiday time from work to help your puppy with this training.

When you leave your puppy alone for a period of time make sure you make this time as good an experience as possible by providing warmth, shelter, fresh water, bedding, some of his toys and something to chew on. Putting some soft music on may help your puppy relax.

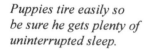

Puppies tire easily so be sure he gets plenty of uninterrupted sleep.

If your puppy can see out to the street it may be best to close the curtains or blinds so he cannot see the street. You don't know who or what may walk past and frighten him, or what frightening sounds he may associate with passers-by, which could lead to fear problems. However, if he can view your back yard through a window this may be better for him as there is less threat from passers-by.

Bedding

Bedding should be warm, dry and comfortable for your puppy. There are many suitable, comfortable dog beds on the market. You will need to find one that suits your puppy. Be aware that puppies will chew, so using bedding that can be chewed without too much damage to the bedding may be a wise choice. Perhaps using second-hand blankets for a while may be best, rather than purchasing any expensive bedding, at least until the puppy is past the chewing stages.

You may want to have two beds for your puppy - one in the living area where he can settle during the day and one for night time next to your own bed so the puppy knows you are around and you can be there if he needs you or needs to go out in the night to relieve himself.

Puppies find it hard to settle when left alone in the dark at night. This would not happen in the wild, nor with his mother or siblings. He needs to know his pack is there for him at any time. He will feel much more secure knowing you are right there for him, day or night. You can also reassure him if he is feeling upset or lonely in the night. With a bit of time, patience and understanding your puppy should settle within a few days.

It may also help your puppy to settle at night if you place a few of his toys with him and also a quality chew or a kong stuffed with nice soft foods he likes. Kongs and chews can be very calming for a puppy and may help him settle more easily. Make sure he also has

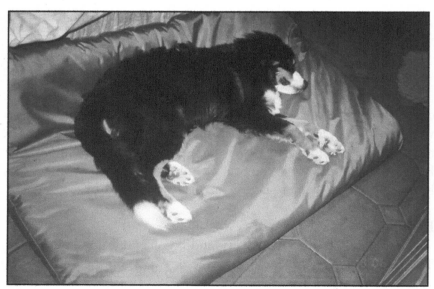

fresh water near his bed. Do not feel if your puppy starts sleeping next to your bed or on your bed that he will be there for life and you will not be able to get him to sleep elsewhere. This is not necessarily true. He can learn to sleep elsewhere by moving his crate or bedding a few inches each night until he is sleeping comfortably where you want him to sleep.

If your puppy makes a mistake

Never shout at or tell your puppy off. Your puppy can not do anything wrong, at least not deliberately. There is no need to shout 'NO' to your puppy as he will not understand this, it may only get him worried, upset or stressed. If he is worried he is not likely to learn and is likely to make more mistakes.

Think about how we feel when we are upset, worried or stressed - it is hard to learn isn't it? It is the same with our puppies. If your puppy makes a mistake, take him gently and calmly out of the situation. Never grab or shake your puppy by the scruff. Wild or domestic dogs only grab their prey by the scruff in an attempt to harm by shaking its neck.

A mother will not do this to her puppies. If we do grab our puppy by the scruff we may be sending the message that we mean him harm. This could have a devastating effect on your relationship with your puppy. If you want to pet your puppy, stroke him gently and slowly. If you find it difficult to stroke gently and slowly, using the back of your hand may help.

How to hold a puppy

If you do need to pick up your puppy, place one arm around the back of his legs to support his bottom and the other arm around his chest to support his front - not under his belly, as this puts pressure on his delicate internal organs, and not by his neck as this also places pressure on his vertebrae which may also cause harm. You can also hold your puppy with one arm around his bottom and allowing him to rest his front paws on your shoulder, with your other hand supporting his back.

When lifting into a car, have the puppy place his front paws on the car, as in the picture on the next page, while you place one

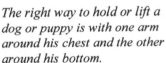

The right way to hold or lift a dog or puppy is with one arm around his chest and the other around his bottom.

arm around his chest and the other arm around his bottom, and lift.

Feeding your puppy

Your puppy should be fed three or four meals a day unless otherwise instructed by your veterinarian. Your breeder should have given you information on how much to feed (which will depend on the breed) and what he has been eating up until purchase.

It is not unusual for a puppy to become a little loose with diarrhoea in his first day or two in his new home. This could be due to the fact

18

that he is now drinking different water and even though his food may be the same as the breeder fed him, it could be prepared a little differently and can still put a little stress on his digestive system, along with the stress of settling into a new home.

Sometimes if a puppy is a little worried or for other reasons, he may go off his food. Don't panic, just have him checked by your veterinarian and ask him/her about the best type of food for your puppy.

Much of the glucose your puppy's body converts from the food he eats is utilised by his brain unless his body is compromised by stress. This is one of the reasons placing your puppy on to the correct diet is important, especially during his growth stages (up to about a year old).

His brain is sensitive to any biochemical or nutritional deficiencies and imbalances of nutrients in his body, influencing his behaviour, thoughts, emotions and how he learns and reacts in different situations.

Correct diet can help restore nutritional balance to the puppy's brain and body systems, which may help in correcting behaviour, how he reacts to situations, how he thinks and learns; and also helps to promote good all-round health and appearance.

A good quality complete life stage dog food should be balanced, providing all the nutrients needed for your growing, developing puppy. Adding human food to an already balanced complete food may upset the balance, which could have serious consequences to his growth and development. However, if you are planning to feed a natural, home-made diet, it may be worthwhile speaking to your veterinarian or canine nutritionist for guidance on the best home-prepared diet for your puppy. Your veterinarian may recommend yearly blood testing to assess the health state of your puppy and make sure he is getting all the nutrients needed in his diet.

Your first veterinary check will give you an opportunity to discuss with your veterinarian your puppy's diet, vaccination and worming programmes and the best treatments to avoid parasites and any other health issue of concern to you.

It is also a good time once you have visited the veterinarian to talk to your breeder and discuss how your puppy is settling in. Remember, you should have plenty of help and support from your breeder, your dog club and your veterinarian.

Teething

Your puppy will go through a period of teething within a few weeks of bringing him home. This is when he will begin to lose his baby teeth and adult teeth start to push through. This begins at around four months of age and although he should have the majority of his adult teeth by the time he is six to seven months of age, he may continue to teethe right up until he is around 12 months of age as it takes longer for his larger molars to come through. During these times of teething he will experience pain which can cause the puppy to chew to relieve the pain.

You can help your puppy out in many ways such as placing some of his toys or a stuffed kong into the refrigerator and giving them to him cold to help cool the gums. You can also place his stuffed

Providing your puppy with his own toys may help prevent him chewing things that he shouldn't chew.

kong into the freezer making it very cold, thus keeping his gums colder for a longer time. Bonjela, used to numb the gums of human babies, is also effective in helping to numb the gums of puppies.

Be patient and never shout at your puppy for chewing. If he is teething, he cannot help it and may be in pain. With a little time and patience the teething phases will eventually pass.

Preparation for puppy class

Speak to a good training centre that can help you prepare for the puppy's arrival, before you bring him home. The trainers can explain which equipment to use and the best time to start the puppy's education programme.

A good training centre should be one that uses positive training methods with a good understanding of canine communication and calming signals. Puppies should not be left playing freely with one another where they can bully each other or become victims, with no-one to protect them in the free-for-all or when they begin to bark or become tired, frantic or stressed. Puppies should never be forced into a situation they are not comfortable with. If this is happening in a class, it generally means the puppies are not coping too well.

However, play is a part of socialisation if it is done correctly with supervision, intervention and stopping the play when necessary. This may be after only a few minutes or just a few seconds, when the play changes from calm rough-and-tumble to quick, frantic play, chasing, barking, growling and biting. This would be a good time to intervene and stop the play.

The classes should create an enriched environment, where the puppies can cope and both puppy and owner can learn in a calm, relaxed, non-threatening atmosphere. There should be escape routes for the puppies if they need to get out of a situation they feel uncomfortable with. Escape routes are important as they help your puppy feel more secure in the environment. It is not natural for puppies to be confined or trapped in unfamiliar or what could be to him, a scary place, without knowing how he can get away if need be. Without escape routes he may feel trapped or worried which can lead to stress and behaviour problems.

The training centre should be willing to help you prepare for your new puppy, after all, it makes the job of the trainers just that much easier when the puppy comes to their classes later on if everyone knows what to expect on the first visit and what equipment and treats to bring.

Whether outdoors or indoors you can take the opportunity to provide an enriched environment.

Your puppy could even visit the training centre if possible beforehand, with no other puppies around, so that he will be familiar with the location and the trainers, and will feel more relaxed when classes begin.

Chapter three

What equipment should I use?

There seems to be a lot of controversy today over which training equipment is the best to use on our puppies and which equipment works the best, what causes pain and what does not. However, have we thought about asking our dogs which equipment they prefer? When we observe our puppies on this issue, they will tell us through their body language.

I have found that the best way to find out if a piece of equipment causes pain for our puppies is to try it on my own arm first. If it hurts, then I certainly would not want to place that piece of equipment on my precious puppy's delicate body. I have seen many dogs die young with suspected neck-related and spine-related health issues and it is possible that check chains were a contributing factor to the health issues of many of these dogs.

Consultations I have conducted with a large number of dogs with problems have shown that they either had painful equipment used on them or something else really unpleasant had happened that they associated with people, children or other dogs. The equipment appears to work in the short term because it shocks the dog out of doing something wrong, but can cause greater problems long-term.

Dogs learn by association. What the puppy experiences at the time of something pleasant or unpleasant happening (something the puppy was seeing, smelling, tasting, hearing or feeling) can stay with him and completely alter the way he regards that particular object or person. For example, a dog when first experiencing a check chain that inflicts pain on the neck when tugged by the handler, may

receive such an unpleasant shock that he begins to associate the pain with children, or other dogs, or whatever he may have been looking at, smelling or hearing when he accidentally or deliberately received the check or tug.

He then may make the association that the children or other dogs have caused the pain and start to bark and lunge to keep them away. Finally, he may become so defensive that he may attack or bite.

Choosing the right training equipment that has the least likely chance of doing your puppy any harm or causing pain is a good start to building a trusting relationship with him. If you are not sure that a piece of equipment is harmful, think about whether or not it is hurting your puppy or making him feel uncomfortable. If you answer yes, then it is most likely doing your puppy harm as well as jeopardising your relationship with him.

There is a large amount of good, humane training equipment on the market today such as wide, soft, flat collars and well-fitted flat, soft harnesses. A collar should cover at least two of your puppy's vertebrae in order to reduce any damage to the neck area and should be soft or preferably padded. Fine collars or chains can easily get in between the vertebrae and may cause damage to the puppy's spine

25

or cause other health problems. The optic nerve runs down the side of the neck, so the eyesight can be affected by pressure in this area.

If you have a puppy that pulls on its lead it may be better to change to a flat, well-fitted harness - at least for a while - until your puppy learns not to pull through using positive, kind training methods. This will help minimise the damage to the puppy while he is being trained. Once you have the puppy walking on a slack lead you can then go back to a wide, soft collar if you like, unless your puppy likes the harness, which many of them come to prefer.

Importance of correct equipment

A long lead is important, to allow your puppy to make optimum use of all his senses while out walking through sniffing, exploring and investigating. A two-metre lead is a good start as it keeps within the legal lead length in some countries, but check the laws of your country and if you are allowed a longer lead on your puppy then use it longer if you wish.

The longer the lead the better for your puppy, as long as the environment is safe. If the area is safe you may also want to give the puppy an opportunity to experience a few minutes off-lead, as long as he will come back to you when called. However, a long lead is often not practical while walking along a footpath beside a busy road or where there is danger - adjust lead length to the environment.

Consider the use of a harness for walking as a long-term option. Most puppies will accept a harness, with the odd exception, such as a touch-sensitive puppy or a puppy with certain skeletal problems. Although a harness will not stop your puppy pulling, it may over time cause the least damage to your puppy's body if he is pulling.

The harness strap width should cover at least two vertebrae, should be well fitted, soft and padded for optimum comfort for the puppy. If you are not sure if the harness fits correctly use your hand as a guide. If you cannot get at least four fingers under the harness, then it is too tight. If you can fit one or two hands under the harness, then it is too loose. If you can get four fingers comfortably under the harness, then it should be a good fit.

Using a long lead

Using a long lead is more preferable than a short lead. About two metres long is a good workable length. You can always shorten it a little if walking along a roadside. They can be a little difficult to use at first but you will soon adjust and your puppy will also learn quickly how to step out if the lead goes between his legs.

When walking your puppy, the walk should be an enjoyable one. Don't make your puppy walk on a short lead, keeping up with your walking pace. Allow your puppy to walk at a slow pace on a long lead, so he has an opportunity to sniff and explore the environment. This will be more enjoyable for him and more mentally stimulating than just a straight, long walk from A to B.

When a puppy uses his senses he is taking in a lot of information, he is reading the daily post (so to speak) - who has been there, what has been there, why they were there and so much more information that we humans do not know about and can not easily comprehend. A puppy can not experience so much when he is on a short or tight lead. Short leads generally leave the puppy no option but to pull. When the puppy pulls, often the handler pulls back, then the puppy pulls more and a tug-of-war problem develops between dog and owner.

It is not necessary for a puppy to walk in the heel position, as this can contribute to health problems. Does your puppy really need to heel? Perhaps a puppy walking well on a loose lead is really what you want. Never yank on the lead or pull your puppy's head up, even if he is wearing a flat, soft collar, as this may have serious health implications. Give your puppy plenty of lead, allowing him to go out exploring to the end of the lead if he wishes.

I can not stress this enough, so again, when walking your puppy, make the walk an enjoyable one. Try not to walk him on a short lead, making him keep up with your walking pace. A short lead gives your puppy little choice but to pull as he has little or no space to communicate with his environment, explore or sniff.

Allowing him to explore will be more enjoyable for the puppy, more mentally stimulating and he will use more energy than just a straight walk, after all, the walk is for the puppy so let him enjoy it and use all his senses doing so. If you want to go on a long, fast walk, please leave your puppy at home.

Laws and owner responsibilities

Many councils require that a puppy has the name and address of the owner on his/her collar. Look into the laws of dog ownership in your area and country. Some countries have a registration or license and microchipping requirement. Some areas allow only a limited number of dogs in a household. In some areas dogs are allowed in cities and on buses or trains, while in other areas they are not.

It is also against the law for your puppy to foul in a public place and leave it there. It is your responsibility as the owner to pick it up. It is always best to carry a few little doggy pick-up bags with you. Your puppy can sometimes go more than once, especially if he gets a little worried.

Dog theft is also a big problem and this is not limited to certain breeds, although in the shooting and hunting seasons gun dog breeds may be targeted. Keep your puppy safe and try not to advertise the fact that there is a puppy in your home by placing your breed stickers in obvious public viewing places, or keeping your puppy in a place where he can be viewed by passers-by.

It is your responsibility to make sure your puppy is provided with a safe, secure home and adequate protection, with daily food, plenty of fresh water to drink, shelter and warmth.

How puppies communicate

Puppies are born with a highly designed communication system. You see this system at work in puppies as young as just a few days old. Given the right opportunity and environment in life, that communication system will continue to develop along with confidence and good social skills.

This dalmatian puppy is communicating strong calming signals: sitting, head turning, slight paw lift.

29

We know that puppies communicate with each other and humans through sound, scent, body and facial expressions, and movement - collectively known as calming signals. Puppies are excellent at reading the facial expressions and body postures of one another, as well as those of humans.

They are always reading our body language and soon recognise what mood we are in by our body language, smell and tone of voice. It is important that we learn how puppies communicate with each other so that we can understand, help them out and meet their daily needs better by using this same communication.

Sound communication

Sound is one of the five senses of puppies. There are many different sounds and tones a puppy can make such as barking, growling, howling, yelping, whining, whimpering and moaning.

These sounds are used as calming signals and puppies will use them to express to humans or other dogs how excited, stressed or worried they are about a situation. However, some dogs may groan if they are enjoying something.

These Labrador puppies are uncomfortable in this situation, displayed by a series of calming signals: sitting, panting, yawning and head turning.

Yawning - Puppies as young as a few days old will display calming signals. They will often use calming signals when they are handled. Many newborn puppies use yawning to inform those handling them that they are not comfortable.

By yawning he is communicating that he is a little worried

with this and is trying to calm the situation down and show that he wants to be placed back into his familiar surroundings. Much of this communication system will develop by what they learn in the

litter as they grow, and from their mother. A puppy at the veterinary clinic may begin to whine and yawn very vocally. Yawning is not always due to tiredness - the puppy is most likely feeling quite stressed in the situation and asking for your help. It may be worthwhile leaving him in the car (if it is safe to do so) while you go in alone and wait to be called into the consultation room before bringing your puppy into the clinic. If there are many dogs in the waiting room it may be better for your puppy if you can use an alternative entry, away from other dogs.

Barking - Barking is natural for puppies, they are born to bark and it is used in communication such as telling others to go away, when stressed, excited, fearful or worried and to stop any potential conflict. They should be allowed to bark a little and it should not develop into a problem in the life of a normal, well-balanced puppy.

A mother with puppies may growl as a warning to her puppies to

31

calm down or she may bark to warn her puppies of danger in which case the puppies will run back to the safety of the den. A puppy may whine and whimper if left alone or if he is in pain or distress. He may moan with pleasure if rubbed around the ears or some other part of his body where he may enjoy being petted.

Never punish or growl at a puppy for barking. There is usually a good reason if a puppy is barking continuously and if you are yelling at him for doing so, he may see your yelling as joining in his barking and his behaviour may increase. He may also feel threatened by your shouting, which may be harmful to your relationship with your puppy. It may be more helpful to cause a distraction to break his focus and take him out of the situation until you find out the reason for his barking and you will then be able to help him.

Barking can be a cry for help and it is up to you as the owner to find out why he is barking and what you can do to help him. It may be that the puppy is in some sort of distress, lonely, worried or not coping with a particular situation and needs your help. If the barking becomes a problem it could be a good time to see a good behaviourist before things get worse.

Scent communication

There are many ways in which a puppy uses scent to communicate. When greeting one another they curve around, sniffing the anal area, taking in all the information they can, learning about each other from chemical messages received. These chemical messages are called pheromones which are produced by both males and females and are present in their urine, faeces, saliva, the pads of their feet and in their anal glands.

Excreting - The urine and faeces of puppies can provide information on the health state, emotional state, whether male or female, and individuals can be recognised by their smells. Sometimes puppies will use urinating as a stress release when

a little worried about a situation. Sometimes they will use urination as a social interaction. This is when you will see many puppies relieve themselves on the same spot. This is often just a social event and we should not read any more into it.

Saliva - If a female has puppies she will lick her puppies' faces with her saliva to place her own smell on their bodies, then she will lick her teats, so they can find their way to her for nursing. This is the first imprinting of the mother's smell on her puppies. For the puppy that cannot yet see, scent is its most life-saving sense. If puppies could not find their way to their mother to nurse, they would die.

Puppies may froth at the mouth when uncomfortable or stressed. They may also use saliva for bonding by licking and grooming one another and their humans.

Sniffing - Sniffing the ground also helps puppies find their way back to their owner when out for a walk, to find treats, or to track food

for survival in the wild. They will leave their own scent on the ground through glands in their paws or through excreting wherever they go and use this scent to find their way back.

Sometimes puppies will use ground sniffing as a calming signal. When they are unsure about something or someone, or other dogs, they may be a little worried and will sniff the ground to help themselves cope with the situation, but you will

most likely see that the eyes are looking around, keeping a watch on things while the nose is down sniffing.

They will sniff both ground and air during times of exploration. Puppies love to use their noses for exploration of new places, investigation or curiosity and can read and learn a huge amount through their noses when given the opportunity to do so.

Body and facial communication

Puppies have a vast variety of body and facial signals that display their emotional, physical and physiological state. If we observe their body language we can learn just how they use their head, eyes, ears, mouths, stance, hair, and tail to communicate.

The face is an important means by which they communicate calming signals. By observing the face and the whole body of your puppy you can begin to understand much about the puppy's needs and what signals or communication he prefers.

He may use many or just one or two calming signals to communicate, but by watching for these signals you can begin to understand when your puppy is communicating his needs.

The following is a list of just some of the calming signals your puppy may use to communicate with other animals or humans when he is feeling stressed, excited, aroused, fearful, worried or threatened. These signals are:

Turning the head	Blinking eyes
Lip licking	Scratching
Turning around	Lungeing
Shaking	Barking
Lifting a paw	Freezing
Sitting	Walking slowly

Whining
Lying down
Splitting up
Panting
Sitting
Play bow
Stiff legs

Yawning
Wagging tail
Sniffing
Frothing at the mouth
Urinating
Head dipping

Sitting, head tilting.

Lip licking, sitting, one puppy lying down and using the other as a barrier.

Heads turning, space between, sitting and soft eyes.

It may appear that everything a puppy does is a calming signal. This is almost true. This is because they are continually communicating unless they are asleep (even then I wouldn't be surprised if they were using calming signals in their dreams). Puppies have been created with an amazing communication system built into them, and from birth they begin to use this system. Dogs blind from birth will also use these calming signals.

As your puppy's owner you can learn to use many of these

35

calming signals to communicate with your puppy. He will be pleased to see you using them and it will help you and your puppy to better understand one another.

If you ignore these signals your puppy may become stressed as he is unable to communicate his needs or get his message through. He will then start to react with displacement behaviour such as biting the lead, jumping up, pulling clothes, being destructive and many more problems. If this displacement behaviour is ignored or punished then the only communication left for the dog is to growl or bite. Growling and biting are used by your puppy only as a last attempt to communicate that he can not cope and needs your help.

Observe your puppy and you will begin to see his calming signals and what he is trying to tell you when using them.

Puppies are peace keepers

Puppies are peace keepers. They try to avoid conflict with humans or other dogs. Conflict is generally only used as a last resort in a desperate situation. Without some knowledge of how puppies communicate, we are very limited in our understanding of what our puppy is trying to tell us, how he may be feeling, what he likes and doesn't like, his needs, when to take him out of a situation and when he is afraid or insecure and needing help.

One example of a puppy splitting up to avoid a conflict between two people is when he goes between partners. Two people may be sitting on a sofa quite close to one another, then suddenly the puppy jumps up and goes between the couple. This behaviour is often mistaken for jealousy but, in fact the puppy is most likely splitting up a potential conflict.

Puppies are born natural conflict solvers. Another example of conflict solving and keeping peace is when two puppies move too close together, then a third dog (usually a mature dog) would go in between to split up what could become a potential conflict.

As their humans we can use this same behaviour with our puppies by walking between them to split up and calm a situation. If you have purchased two puppies together or have two young dogs in your household, you may need to do a lot of splitting up and going between them to calm them down until they are mature.

It is not normal for puppies or adult dogs to hug each other by placing their paws over each other making contact the way humans do. When humans place their arms over or around puppies, they will often see this form of contact as threatening and a potential for conflict. Usually you will see some calming signals from the puppies, such as head dipping, lip licking or yawning. This is body language that tells us the puppy is not comfortable with this human behaviour.

If there is a another dog around you may see this dog go between in order to calm the situation and prevent conflict.

This is the same in a multi-dog household when a family member

Dog behind the owner has turned its back on the other dogs and the owner has intervened by stepping between them, to help them cope.

pets one puppy, another puppy may rush over and go between, in order to prevent a potential conflict and calm the situation down. This is an attempt by the puppy to keep the peace in his home, by preventing any conflict that may occur when people or other animals get too close.

Nose work for your puppy

Puppies love to sniff and explore. We need to be aware of our puppy's amazing abilities and his need to use his senses. Your puppy was born to use his five senses. Allowing puppies to explore, sniff and taste different safe objects helps their development. However, be careful not to overload your puppy with too much or he may become too overwhelmed and shut down. Not more than 10 minutes, once or twice a day is enough for a small puppy.

Give your puppy some pet toys or safe household junk such as old shoes, slippers, socks, clothes, handbags, fruit, vegetables, plants, hay, old toys etc., scattered around a room or garden for him to explore. You can even use an old cardboard box and hide some

An enriched environment helps puppies develop their exploration skills and build confidence.

yummy treats in it or under some of the other objects, or make a tent out of a chair and old blankets.

Use your imagination and be creative. If he is investigating an

38

object that is not doing him any harm, then allow him to do so. Give him the space and opportunity to explore, as this will help his development.

This nose work will cost him more energy than a long walk (even just a few minutes) - it is hard work for the puppy but it is a necessary part of his development.

Many insecurity problems develop in puppies through their lack of self-confidence, so do not stop him from using his senses. Do not allow him to chase anything - keep him on a long lead. If he is in a safe and secure environment, you can allow him a little time off lead but place him back on lead if you anticipate that he is about to chase anything.

The more he is allowed to chase, the better he will become at chasing and the more likely he will develop chase behaviour you do not want such as chasing cars, cyclists, joggers etc. It is very hard to stop this behaviour once it is well established.

New environment

In a new environment your puppy will first look to see what is around him, taking information through his eyes, and then the head goes down and he will start to take in the information through his nose.

Taking your puppy to any new environment can be scary. He will need to explore and check it out, he will need to know it is safe and a pleasant place to be.

Never train a puppy in a new environment. He will not be able to concentrate until he has established that the area is safe through exploration. Allow him to sniff and investigate the area before beginning any training or activity.

The puppy needs to sniff and explore so he knows what is in his environment. Allowing him to do what he was born to do and understanding his needs is the beginning of a wonderful relationship with your puppy.

A scary object

Some objects can be scary, especially for puppies. Allow your puppy to walk up to, and explore, any object in his own time and in his own way without pushing or rushing him. Our pushy intervention can do more harm than good in this situation.

If the puppy wants to go away from the scary object, then allow him to do so. It is okay for him to walk away, he may be ready to deal with it another day.

Giving him the choice to walk away will help him to feel more secure, knowing he can leave if things feel a little scary for him.

Using a barrier

A long lead is most helpful when a puppy is afraid, as he has the opportunity to choose to leave the immediate area if he needs to, or hide behind his owner or a nearby tree, parked car, hedge, gateway or other barrier to help him cope with the situation.

If the puppy is indoors, make sure he is aware of the exit doors (escape routes) and leave them open if possible, allowing him to go outside if need be, providing it is secure outdoors, otherwise place him on a long lead or house-line.

Chapter four

How puppies learn

Your puppy begins to learn from the moment he is born. He learns to suckle and he learns the smell of his own mother as she imprints her smell on him by licking his little body then her own teats. The puppy follows the saliva scent of his mother to find the teats to suckle.

During the first few weeks he learns to play with litter mates and he learns that the den is a safe place. All this helps towards his development and learning. However, for his brain to develop to its full potential he needs to interact within the environment in the outside world (outside the den or bed area). As your puppy grows he needs gentle, positive exposure to different environments such as sounds, other mature dogs, different types of people and nose work.

When your puppy is given opportunity to use his nose, brain and senses, his brain will be developing along with confidence and independence. But do not overwhelm him with too much or he may shut down and little will be learned. About 10 minutes a day is sufficient for a small puppy up until about 16 weeks, depending on the puppy and the breed. The time can be increased a little as the puppy grows older.

Puppies do not generally cope well with too much activity or if they are not given enough rest or sleep, too much noise around them or placing them in a scary environment, or any other situation in which your puppy may not feel comfortable. Giving your puppy any bad experiences at this young age can stay with him for life.

Stress will affect the learning process and just like humans find it hard to learn under stress, so do puppies. Remember to watch for the calming signals and if you feel your puppy is not coping well, take him out of the situation. Good experiences will help him to cope better later in life.

Exercise

Exercise is important for good physical health. It is good for keeping the muscles toned as muscles develop through movement, and it helps to keep internal organs in a healthy state and functioning well. However, too much exercise can be just as harmful as too little. The correct amount of exercise will depend on your dog and breed.

Exercise should be done in a safe, non-threatening environment so the experience is good, such as a forest, park, visiting a friend's house, walking around a lake or on country walkways etc. City streets can be quite frightening, often polluted, busy and noisy which can be a little too overwhelming and threatening for a puppy. There will be plenty of time when he is a little older to slowly become used to the constant rush of the city life.

If your only option is to walk your puppy around the streets it may be best to choose walking times when the streets are most quiet, such as dawn or dusk. If your puppy has a frightening experience when out on a walk he may associate the experience with the environment and not want to go there again.

If possible try walking him in the quieter streets first, building up his time among traffic little-by-little as he ages. Try to make the walk pleasant and enjoyable by allowing him to explore and praise him for doing it. Allow him to take whatever time he needs. If he starts to show a lot of calming signals take him out of the situation and reduce the time walking near traffic on his next walk. Try not to rush by placing him among busy traffic too soon or you may frighten him and set back his training.

If you see other dogs or people walking towards you, watch your puppy's calming signals and take him out of the situation by crossing the road or going in a different direction. Sometimes parked cars, fences or trees can be used as a barrier to help the puppy when passing.

How much exercise

Your puppy will need very little exercise during the first few months of life, especially if he is a large breed that can be susceptible to hip problems. A good guide for how much exercise

is enough would be to begin with a five minute walk from when the puppy is about four months old and build up by five minutes a month until the dog is walking for about 40 minutes a day by the time he is 12 months old.

Forty minutes of slow, calm walking once a day should be plenty of exercise for an adult dog but again this depends on the dog and breed. It could be too much for some dogs, or not quite enough for others.

A good indication as to whether your puppy has had enough exercise is how he reacts after the walk. If he cannot settle and looks as if he wants more exercise, then he has probably had too much. The walk may have been too long or too fast for him or he may have had too much play with other dogs, or too much ball chasing.

Next time decrease the walk a little by not walking so far or so fast and not allowing your puppy to engage in so much play, but instead give a little nose work (finding treats, sniffing etc). Just like a child that has become overtired and cannot settle down after too much activity, this can also happen to puppies when they have had too much exercise.

If your puppy can settle and rest after a walk then you have most likely given him a nice, relaxing, calm walk that has been about the right length of time.

A fast or long walk is not going to be as enjoyable for your puppy as much as a nice calm stroll, taking in the sounds, sights and smells and allowing him the opportunity to explore.

Sleep

Your puppy will need a lot of rest and it will seem he is always resting and sleeping for most of the day. This is perfectly fine. Do not attempt to wake him or disturb him when he is sleeping. Your puppy will need around 18-20 hours of sleep a day so give him the time and space to do so. Make sure he has his own bed or crate that he can go into whenever he needs to sleep or rest.

When he puts himself to bed, leave him to rest and do not allow anyone to wake him. Children are especially good at disturbing and waking puppies, which may create stress for him when he needs to sleep. Educate children to leave the puppy if he puts himself to bed or if he is sleeping anywhere. Your puppy needs to know he is safe and protected by his owners in his own bed and home area.

Play

In the litter, puppies will play with one another. This play with the supervision of their mother helps them to learn about relationships and how to be polite and sociable. They will also learn important life skills from one another and their mother, such as bite inhibition.

A good mother will teach them when to stop playing, as she will intervene if play gets too rough or too much for the puppies. She will do this by splitting them up. This is a skill she will use to calm the puppies, we can also use this skill to calm or split up our own puppy when play gets out of hand with other puppies or dogs.

Play should be kept to a minimum for your puppy. Play can be quite stressful, especially if it goes on for more than a few minutes. This is why puppy parties must be supervised and intervention used when it becomes too much for them, which is usually within a few minutes of play (sometimes it takes only a few seconds, depending on the puppy).

During these times of play puppies do not always learn what we expect them to learn. Often what they are learning is how to growl

45

and bite one another, bully others, chew other dogs and people, bark at each other and people, become fearful when they cannot get out of a situation (escape routes), body slam, run away, chase, wrestle, become victims, not listen to owners (they are often too stressed to listen) and much more unwanted behaviour that can affect them for the rest of their lives.

Your puppy is born with many instincts and one of those instincts is to hunt. Chasing, tug-of-war and tearing are part of that hunting instinct (in some breeds it is stronger than others). This means that when you throw a ball or any other object, or play tug with your puppy, he may tug or chase whether he wants to or not.

The muscles become active within the puppy at the sight of the object moving. This muscle action is triggered by the limbic system of the brain as soon as the puppy sees the object moving.

So in fact your puppy may not be able to control his chase instinct when something moves. He may chase or bite it because the instinct to do so is there and he has little control over those instincts, especially if we have encouraged them to kick-in through a lot of play.

Some puppies may learn from their mother not to chase a ball or other objects or play tug. It is best not to force or teach your puppy to chase or play tug games, as once the chase instinct has kicked in and your puppy is chasing or tugging any object you throw, he may find it hard to distinguish between his ball or toys moving and anything else moving such as cars, cyclists, runners, children playing, sheep or other animals.

This instinct may put your puppy's life in danger and the problem could be almost impossible to stop once it has started, so it is best to prevent it in the first place by finding other ways to channel your time with your puppy, such as encouraging nose work and brain work games.

Quality time with your puppy

There are many ways in which you can spend time with your puppy, bonding and developing a good relationship. Following is a list of things you and your puppy can do together:

Massage your puppy – Using gentle light massage, stroke your dog with very slow movements starting at the head and moving slowly down your puppy's body.

This should take about 10 seconds to get from top of his head to his tail on a medium sized puppy. Do this for about 20 minutes a day for the first week if your puppy is comfortable - otherwise less time, depending on what your puppy will allow - about 15 minutes a day for the second week and then five to 10 minutes a day for the dog's entire life.

This is a great way to assist bonding between you and your puppy. You will also learn about your puppy's body, whether there are changes in body temperature or in coat or skin texture.

You should also notice if there is a change in smell to his breath, body or ears, so you can attend early to anything that may need medical attention.

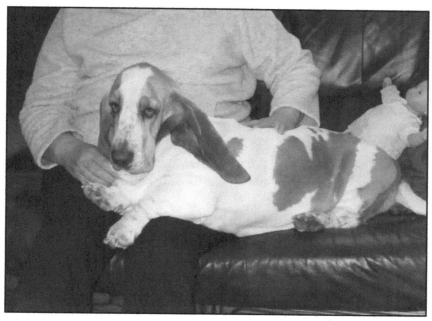

Retrieve treat object - You can use many things for this game. An old empty container or bottle, a toy specifically made for this game, or anything you can place a few treats into that your puppy cannot get the treats out of.

The game is played by placing treats into the container and closing the lid. Let your puppy see you place the treats into the container then hide the container.

Your puppy can then be encouraged to find the container. When he finds the container, praise him, open the lid and take out a treat and give to him (pretend to eat one yourself so your puppy thinks he is sharing with you).

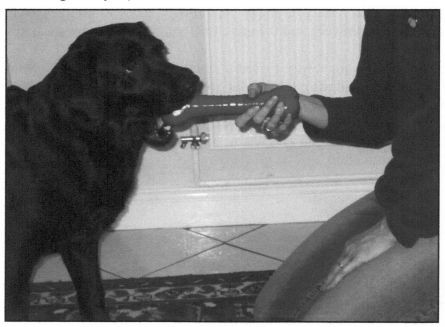

Close the lid and hide the container again. This time allow your puppy to move a step or two towards you before you open the lid and share a treat with him.

Build up the distance of the retrieve one or two steps at a time (over a few days or weeks depending on the dog) and you should be able to hide the container anywhere and your puppy will find it and bring it to you for sharing.

This game is very interactive and relationship building.

Nose work – Puppies enjoy nose work games. Hide toys or treats such as hotdog sausages, small pieces of fruit or vegetables, cooked meat or anything your puppy really likes (provided it is safe and he

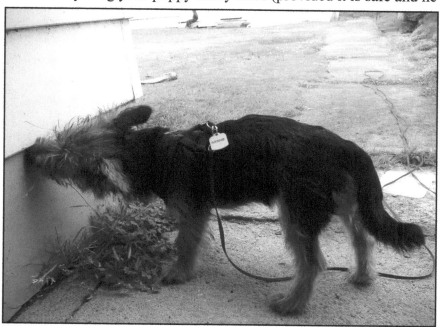

is not allergic). Start indoors and then move to outdoors around your property or in a forest or park.

Do not show your dog where the treats are but just say *find* and leave your puppy to find the treats - his nose will tell him where they are without any help from you.

You can also throw a few treats such as dry biscuits or cut up sausages, into long grass and tell him to *find*. Your puppy will love these games as he is doing what he is born to do, that is to use his nose.

Nose work games are very mentally stimulating, helping him to think and use his brain. This work will be very tiring, so he will need plenty of rest after playing these games. Keep it limited to just a few minutes a day when you are dealing with young puppies that tire easily.

Brain work games - There are many brain work games you can play together, some of which can be purchased and some you can create yourself. One game that can be purchased is a board game with blocks of wood. Your puppy learns to take out the blocks to find the treat underneath. As he becomes better at this game you can

reduce the number of blocks that have treats hidden underneath.

Your puppy uses his nose to sniff out which blocks hide the treats and only checks under those blocks to receive his reward. There is a small hole at the top of each block so the puppy can sniff out the treats.

Enrich your puppy's environment - Indoors and outdoors, with plenty of toys and things he is allowed to play with, chew up and destroy if he wants to.

They must be things that are safe such as old shoes, slippers, toys (hard and soft), cardboard boxes, old containers or bottles (you can put treats in these), paper, plants to smell, hay, make tunnels out of chairs and blankets etc, anything to make your dog's environment enriched, fun and safe. Use plenty of creativity.

Kong - This can be stuffed with yummy food your puppy enjoys. When stuffed, you can give it to him right away or you can place it in a freezer and give it to your puppy frozen (especially if he is teething), but some dogs prefer it not frozen. This may keep him occupied for hours and can help with teething by cooling down the mouth and keeping him chewing the kong rather than your furniture.

After eating the food out of it your puppy will be very tired and is likely to sleep for an hour or two. A few suggested treats you can put into the kong are: fish, low fat cream cheese, cottage cheese, meat, peanut butter, mashed potato, your dog's meal, rice, soaked rolled oats, vegetables or any selection of suitable soft moist foods.

If you have a puppy that gulps down his food very fast, it may be

a to serve
inside the

also a very
stress-reducing and
calming activity for
most puppies.

By forcing the puppy
to eat more slowly (he
must work hard to access
food from a kong) you
can also help to prevent
the onset of bloat in
susceptible breeds.

Play balls – This game is done by placing small plastic balls in a large empty container (such as a child's empty paddling pool or sand pit or other large container). You may need to use a very small container for very small puppies.

Fill the container with the balls and place treats in among the

balls. Watch the puppy try and find the treats by pushing balls out of the way and having a great time.

This can also be played by placing a few inches of water in the container and placing a few balls to float on the top. Drop treats into the water and watch your puppy try to get the treats in the water.

Some treats will sink, which is okay - your puppy may also enjoy placing his nose under water to get them, especially if it is a hot day.

Chapter five

Stress and its consequences

Stress can be almost anything that makes our puppies react to a physical, mental or emotional stimulus. What may seem just a small trivial situation to us may be a very serious or fearful situation to our puppy.

With our fast, modern and urban lifestyles (which are no longer very dog friendly), dogs have had to learn to cope with life and situations that are not natural to them.

Puppies can adapt quite well to the routines of our lifestyle, however, what one puppy may cope with, another puppy may not and many puppies will not cope with a busy, fast lifestyle that may have adverse short-term or long-term consequences on his body as he grows and develops.

Many people will understand what causes stress in their own lives but not many of us really see what may be causing stress in the lives of our puppies.

The adrenal glands are responsible for the hormones caused by stress. The adrenal medulla produces adrenalin and noradrenalin which is released if your puppy is stressed.

Short-term stress places the puppy's body into a state of *fight or flight* - placing the puppy into a heightened state of anxiety, fear and awareness. Longer-term stress causes the adrenal cortex to release the hormone cortisol which, when released over a long period of time, takes its toll on the puppy's physical body and emotions which may cause his body to react either in one or in many ways such as those in the list below.

Symptoms of stress
- Unbalanced blood sugar levels
- Insulin resistance
- Weight gain or weight loss
- Lowered immunity
- Increased risk of diseases ending with *'itis* such as pancreatitis, colitis, tracheitis, arthritis etc
- Infections, joint pain, headaches
- Muscle weakness or other health issues
- Using a lot of calming signals, body language
- Red eyes, whites of eyes showing, weeping eyes, dilated pupils
- Fear of people, cowering
- Fear of other dogs or animals
- Destructive behaviour
- Biting or chewing a lot, ankle biting
- Licking paws
- Barking, whining
- Jumping up or pulling at peoples clothes
- Digging or scratching at things
- Bullying or possessiveness
- Growling, becoming grumpy or depressed
- Touch sensitive
- Shadow chasing
- Wanting to play continuously (OCD tendencies)
- Cannot settle or sleep
- Fussy eating, won't take treats
- More than usual amount of hair falling out, alopecia
- Mounting behaviour
- Pulling hard on lead, biting lead
- Dry, brittle or greasy coat, dandruff
- Hiding or using barriers or escape routes to get away
- Jerking movements, pacing or quick-stepping
- Drinking more than usual
- Urinating or defecating more than usual

- High pulse rate, fast heart rate
- Rapid breathing, fast panting
- Hyperactive as more glucose is released into muscles
- Digestive system affected, diarrhoea
- Poor reproduction
- Poor problem solving ability
- Lowered learning ability
- Lowered concentration
- Shut down

Not every symptom on the list above will affect your puppy. It may be that he shows only one or two symptoms or perhaps several. No matter how many symptoms your puppy displays it is never too late to take action and do something about it. Acknowledging the symptoms means you are already half way there to helping your puppy out. You now need to find out why he is showing the symptoms of stress, so that you can take appropriate action.

The list below is not a comprehensive list but just some of the daily issues that may cause your puppy stress.

What might cause stress
- Hunger, thirst
- Too hot, too cold
- Health problems, pain, skeletal
- Female in season
- New environment
- New owner, partner or baby
- Loss of friend, grief
- Family conflict
- Dog-dog conflict
- Meeting strange dogs or people
- Given too many commands
- Being shouted at
- Too much training, aversives used in training
- Training Centres, dog clubs, dog shows, sport events
- Too much exercise, activity, agility, racing, hunting
- Not enough exercise

- Lack of shelter
- Being trapped
- Left in crate for long periods
- Lack of relationship with owners
- Being left alone for long periods
- Lack of toilet opportunity
- New home, country
- Weather, thunder, lightning, storms, rain, wind, heat
- Fireworks
- Busy traffic, busy streets
- Too many people or animals
- Visitors, postman, window cleaner
- Visits to veterinarian, vet nurse, therapist
- Too much noise
- Smells, air fresheners, incense, oils, perfume, DAP
- Children playing, running, screaming
- Playing active games, frisbee, balls, chase, rough-and-tumble
- Poor diet, incorrect diet

Don't be frightened by these lists. It may appear that everything in the puppy's life may cause him stress and it is easy to blame everything on stress. However, only some of the things listed may affect your puppy, just as only some may affect we humans. It depends on the puppy, breed, genetics, state of health, environment and lifestyle, and it depends how you, as the owner, can help your puppy learn to cope with our modern lifestyles.

Just like we humans, when a puppy's stress level is high, his adrenalin level is high too. This adrenalin peaks within around 15 minutes but can take between two and six days to come back down to normal, provided nothing else happens to the puppy in the meantime (such as visitors, meeting strange dogs on a walk, training classes and many more daily events).

There are many things we can do to lower our own stress levels - we can read a book, we can watch television, eat comfort foods, we can go for a calm walk on the beach, country road or park, or we may have an enjoyable relaxing hobby. But what about our puppies, what do we give them to do in order to bring down their daily stress levels? Often we do very little but to take our puppy for a walk which is often another stress added to the daily events.

There are many ways in which you can help your puppy to live a lifestyle that keeps his stress levels down and maintained at a low level in order to help him cope better with life and help avoid any health issues that may arise from a stressful lifestyle.

As your puppy develops more confidence, he will learn to cope better with life. Below is a list (not comprehensive) which may help to reduce or maintain lower stress levels as well as help with confidence building and better coping skills.

Stress reduction techniques
- First take your puppy to visit your veterinarian to rule out any underlying health issues
- Correct diet for your individual puppy, see your veterinarian or canine nutritional therapist. They can also provide you with the correct supplementation for your puppy if need be.
- A canine therapist can help your puppy with any rebalancing through bodywork techniques
- Provide basic needs of warmth, shelter, food, water, toilet opportunity and closeness
- Avoid giving your puppy a high fat, high sugar diet which places strain on the adrenal glands
- Good relationship with your puppy, allowing him to be in the house with you as part of the family, not left alone outdoors
- Involve puppy in calm family activity, not highly active
- Allow your puppy to make his own choices, avoiding commands where possible
- Speaking calmly, use body language rather than saying *NO*, i.e. splitting up, going between, yawning or using other calming signals
- Moving slowly instead of fast
- Curve around your puppy when approaching - don't move directly into his space

- Allow your puppy to approach you, rather than you approaching him
- Nose work and brain work games
- Hide your puppy's treats or meal around your yard or in your house for puppy to find
- Massage, bodywork
- Calm music if your puppy likes it
- Give your puppy blankets, toys or anything else he might like to use for comfort or to play with
- Plenty of rest and sleep during the day and at night
- Never waken your puppy from sleep, especially rem (dreaming) sleep, when you see jerky movements or even barking during sleep.
- Space - your puppy will need his own space
- Using stuffed kongs daily or other types of chews, you can also provide your puppy's meal in the kong provided the meal is moist
- Walking on a long loose lead
- Correct amount of exercise for puppy's age and breed
- Daily short, calm, slow walk, allowing puppy to sniff and explore away from other dogs or humans
- If you want your puppy to walk with other dogs, allow him to walk only with calm, mature dogs he is familiar with.

Chapter six

Training positively

All training with your puppy should be kept short and sessions should be nice, positive and calm experiences. You should never need to raise your voice. If you find yourself getting at all frustrated, end the task and try again another time. Your puppy needs your understanding, patience and support during training sessions.

Puppies have very short concentration spans so please keep the sessions to just a minute or two about two to three times a day. Your puppy will learn much faster and will be much happier if you both enjoy your time together. Remember your puppy will be learning from you and his environment every minute of the day, whether he is in a training session or not.

Punishment is not necessary with puppies and may be seriously damaging to his relationship with you. They do not deliberately do wrong. They are only young and still learning your household rules and what's right, wrong, safe or dangerous.

This will take time for him to learn. Rather than using punishment it is much better for your relationship to teach him the correct behaviour you want through your body language and kind methods of training.

I have not included a *sit* or a *down* among the training tips in this book. That is because your puppy already knows how to sit or down without owners teaching it. If he finds it difficult to *sit* or *down* naturally, then it may be worth having your veterinarian check him over for any possible health problem.

60

If your puppy frequently sits or downs on his own, you have many opportunities to place the behaviour on cue without the need for training sessions or force. Whenever your puppy sits you can tell him to *sit* and whenever he goes down, you can tell your puppy *down*. After pairing the behaviour with the words a number of times, he should soon make the association between the cue words and the behaviour.

Let him know when you are about to start or finish a training session with him. This way he knows what is about to happen and does not have to try and guess what's going on. You may want to use the words *training time* to begin training and the word *finished* when the session is over.

Whatever you use does not matter, as long as your puppy understands what is about to happen. It is also important that you look at your puppy's state of health each day, especially before you begin training.

Dogs have off days too - they have days when they don't feel like training or going out for a walk, they have days during which they are not feeling so well, just as we do.

Be aware of how your puppy may be feeling, look at his calming signals and if you think your puppy is not up to training today it may be best to leave his training until another time when he is feeling up to it.

What treats should be used?

This task can be very helpful before starting your training session with your puppy as you will know the best treats to use for your session. However, what a puppy likes best one day could be different the next day so you may need to do this test on your puppy before each training session.

Take two different treats, place one in the left hand and a different one in the right hand. Close your fists loosely so your puppy can almost get to the treats. Show both fists to your puppy and let him sniff them, keeping your fists apart making it easier for him to distinguish which treat is in which hand.

As he sniffs the treats in your fist, you will see that your puppy may prefer one treat over the other by the way he may keep preferring to sniff at the fist with his favoured treat. You can try this with a few different treats in the same way to determine which treats your puppy might prefer that day during his training sessions.

When giving a treat to your puppy as a reward for good behaviour, make sure the treat is already in your hand. If you are wasting precious seconds trying to get treats out of pockets or bags, it may be too late by the time you give the treat to your puppy. The treat needs to be given to the puppy within 0.8 of a second of the correct behaviour. After this time your puppy's concentration is gone and he is probably thinking of other things and has no idea why he is being rewarded.

Never lean over your puppy when treating him, make sure you treat him side-on. When your puppy approaches you, turn slightly side-on to him so he feels more comfortable with this approach, then crouch down a little and treat from your side, not with stretched out arms and not leaning over the puppy. Your puppy is more likely to be comfortable approaching you if he is not threatened by your behaviour.

Taking your puppy to the veterinarian
Before your puppy meets his veterinarian it will help if you can arrange to take him to the veterinary practice beforehand while no other clients are waiting, just to visit the practice and meet the nurses. Ask the nurses to briefly greet him but not to make a big fuss or he may become suspicious or afraid. Spread a few treats on the

floor or hand treat him if he is not able to be placed on the ground. Stay only about five minutes, then leave.

A few days later go a second time and repeat as for the first visit, but this time have him briefly meet the veterinarian with a treat. Your puppy should begin to see the veterinary practice as a nice place, rather than a threatening place providing all his experiences there are good.

When it is time for him to have any treatment by the veterinarian, have your puppy wait in the car (if safe to do so) while you go in and wait. This will avoid the stress of meeting strange dogs, which can give puppies a fearful association to the veterinary practice and undo all the work you have done. When your puppy is called you may like to ask the veterinarian if you can bring your puppy through another door away from other animals in the waiting room.

Take some treats with you, treat your puppy at the very moment he is being vaccinated. This may distract him from focusing on what the veterinarian is doing.

Providing you make each visit to the veterinarian a good, calm experience for your puppy, he shouldn't develop any fear or behaviour problems associated with the veterinary practice.

Taking your puppy to the groomer

Just as with taking your puppy to the veterinarian you should arrange with your groomer to have your puppy visit when there are no other clients or dogs there if possible. You can have your groomer greet your puppy briefly (and carry on with her normal tasks).

Scatter some treats around the groomers clinic and allow your puppy to sniff and explore the place finding the treats. This will help your puppy make a good association to the place. Have the groomer turn on and off the clippers a few times well away from the puppy. Leave while the puppy is feeling happy and confident. The visit should be no more than five to 10 minutes.

Arrange another visit if possible when the grooming clinic is quiet and take your puppy in again. Do everything as for your first visit, only this time sit on the floor with your puppy and a very soft brush and gently brush him if he will allow you. The groomer can carry on with her work, so the puppy gets used to the sounds and activity of the place. Arrange a third visit on another quiet day, do everything as on your second visit, but this time place your puppy with a chew in one of the crates, just for a few minutes and sit down beside the crate with him. Walk out, wait five seconds and straight back in again. Take your puppy out of the crate and leave.

You may find your puppy is fine with the groomers by this stage, or you may find he needs more visits to build up his confidence. Take your time, a good groomer will understand your puppy's hesitation and allow him to take all the time he requires. After all, he may need to visit the groomer for the rest of his life, so making sure it is a good experience is vital at this stage. If you find any of the stages are too much for your puppy take it back a step or two. Once your puppy is happy and finding the groomer's clinic a nice place to be, he should accept being groomed for the rest of his life.

House training your puppy

This method of house training, sometimes called toilet or potty training, can be taught to puppies or dogs of any age. Of course the sooner the toilet training process is taught the better for everyone. Start the moment your puppy comes into your home. When you bring the puppy home, take him outside into the garden. Wait with the puppy until he does his business. Just as he squats say whatever word you have chosen for his business such as *busy, pee pee*, or *get going*.

I will use the word *busy* as my chosen word here. Say *busy, good boy, busy* and pet the puppy with soft gentle slow strokes on the side of his body once he has finished (not hard or fast strokes or slaps as this is stressful for puppies and may be seen as punishment). Make sure the word chosen is the first word you say and also the last word you say i.e. *busy, good boy, busy*.

A puppy will need to go every hour or two depending on the puppy for those first few months, so there are plenty of opportunities each day to train your puppy to *busy* when you ask him. He will be a little stressed the first couple of days and will need to go outside a little more often than he will once settled into your home.

Your puppy will also need to relieve himself as soon as he wakes from a sleep, just after exercise or play, after drinking and after each meal, so these are good times to take him into the yard to *busy*.

There are also other signs which may indicate your puppy needs to go out for a *busy*. Your puppy may start to circle in the room or he may start to walk a little faster than usual, sniffing the floor. He may even make a little whimper or scratch at the door.

Make sure you take your puppy to *busy* on a variety of different grounds such as grass, concrete, hay, soil, wood chips and many other types of ground you can find so he does not begin to think he is allowed to *busy* on only one type of ground.

Puppies that think they cannot *busy* on other types of ground may hold on all day until they get a chance to *busy* only on the ground that they have been taught to go on. It is very stressful for puppies to hold on all day. Can you imagine a child or even yourself holding on all day?

If the puppy does his *busy* inside the house just ignore it, accidents do happen. Put him gently out of the way while you clean it up and be careful to watch for the signs next time. Do NOT growl, shout, hit the puppy or rub his nose in it. This will only stress him and puppies can not learn properly when they are stressed - he would then be likely to hide from you the next time he wants a *busy*.

Your puppy will learn that doing his *busy* indoors gains no reward as he is ignored for this behaviour. The puppy will learn that doing his *busy* outdoors gets him a wonderful reward of praise, thus increasing the behaviour. From time to time give him a treat when you praise him for doing a *busy* outdoors, but not every time. This helps to reinforce the behaviour you want.

Never rush the puppy in house training. Some may learn in days or weeks, yet some may take months, depending on the puppy, his environment, state of health and the breed. Every puppy learns at a different rate. Be patient and calm and your puppy will learn in due time.

When cleaning up your puppy's mess, it is always best to get rid of the smell completely so he does not return to the same area to make his mess again. There are some ready-made cleaners you can purchase from pet stores or you can use biological soap powder or vinegar that will disguise any smell and prevent him from returning to that place.

Crate training your puppy

Crate training is an excellent way to educate your puppy. He will feel he has his own little space in the house that is especially for him. It will become a personal haven for him if he needs time out to escape from children, family, friends or other dogs or animals in the house.

You can take the crate on holiday with you and your puppy so he has a safe, secure, familiar place to rest. It is also good to use for your puppy travelling in a car. You can use a normal puppy bed for this same task if you do not plan to use a crate.

It is important to understand a little about using a crate before you begin the crate training. Never use the crate or puppy's bed as a place of punishment or a place to put your puppy when you want him out of the way, or he may think of it as a bad place to be and never want to go there. He should never be shut in the crate for long periods of time. A long period of time would depend on your puppy. Every puppy is different and you may find your puppy does not like a crate at all and prefers a bed.

You may find he will learn to cope with only a few minutes at a time in the crate, or he may be happy to sleep or rest in the crate for two to three hours. If for some reason you need him to become used to being shut in for a short time, start with just a few minutes a day giving him something nice in the crate such as a chew or a stuffed kong.

You may also sit beside the crate and read a book or something quietly while your puppy settles in the crate, so he does not feel he is left alone every time he is placed in a crate. Build the time up over many weeks or months until he can cope in the crate for perhaps a couple of hours per day. A puppy should never be shut in a crate all day or even half a day. Think about how you would feel being shut in a small, confined space for much of the day.

If you do need to confine your puppy to a small area while you are away, it may be worth trying a child's large play pen or even using a dog gate in a doorway, confining the puppy to a small room.

These gates are especially helpful in a busy house or a multi-dog household as they give your puppy a little more time and space away from the busy areas of the house or the playfulness and demands of

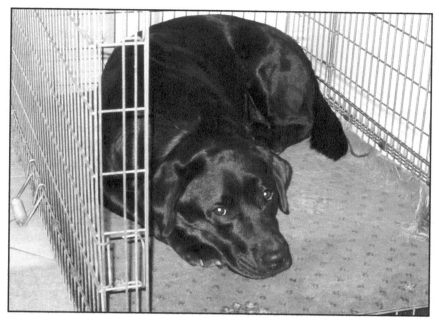

other dogs. You can also place these gates at the bottom of stairs to prevent your puppy going into the rooms upstairs or falling downstairs.

Crate training can be an easy way to house train your puppy. Puppies do not like to relieve themselves in a place where they sleep, eat and play so may hold on as long as possible if shut in a crate. Very young puppies cannot hold on for long periods of time and may relieve themselves in the crate accidentally, which would make the crate not such a rewarding place if the puppy had to sleep in his mess.

Place some paper down in one part of the crate just in case the puppy has to relieve himself. Remove the paper as soon as possible after he has used it and replace it with clean paper. Never leave the puppy in a crate where he has excreted as the discomfort will create much stress for him.

Place the crate in an area of the house that is not too busy or noisy, such as the corner of the kitchen or living room where he can see his family and not feel he is being isolated or punished. The crate should be big enough for the puppy or adult dog to sit, stand, turn around and stretch out.

Leave the crate door open most of the time so the puppy can go in and out of it whenever he wants to rest, sleep, play with his toys or get away into some space of his own. The crate can be covered if need be to help the puppy rest.

Puppies love to have a place of their own to rest and escape from humans or other animals and he will learn to go into the crate when he needs to. Only close the crate door when children or other animals may be disturbing him and he needs to rest. It will prevent children from getting easy access to him and will also prevent accidents around meal times and cooking when a puppy could get under your feet when you are carrying hot food.

Feed your puppy his meals in his crate and place a small bowl of water nearby, or just inside the crate so he feels that it is his special place filled with many rewards. There are special non-spill bowls you can purchase from pet stores, however, some puppies have been known to tip even these ones. But it's worth a try as they are great for inside the crate, especially if you are taking the puppy anywhere for a long distance in your car.

Never force the puppy to go into the crate. If he sees the crate as a rewarding place and a place where he is left in peace when he needs time out, then he will be more likely to go in the crate when you ask him to. Every time he goes into the crate use your own chosen word, such as *in the crate* or *in your bed*.

When you are eating your own meals give your puppy a chew or kong type toy stuffed with food in his crate, so he feels that when you eat, he gets a special treat of his own, which may keep him from begging at your table. Do not throw food to your dog when you eat at the table - it may take only one little treat from your table and he could beg for the rest of his life. If your dog learns to use those adorable puppy eyes you may not be able to resist.

Once your puppy is happily going into his crate for his food and rest you may be able to shut him in for a few hours overnight if you need to. Make sure you take your puppy out to relieve himself just before you go to bed and then let him out again as soon as you get up in the morning.

If he is unsettled during any part of the night it may be that you need to take him out to relieve himself. There may be a mess in the crate to clean up every morning for a while as he learns control.

The overnight control may take days, weeks or months, depending on the dog. All dogs are different and just because the neighbour's dog had overnight control in a few days does not mean your puppy will do the same. Be patient and never leave your puppy shut in the crate for long periods. Allow him to have the choice of going into the crate when he wants to and staying there as long as he wants to with the door open so he has access to come and go.

Car familiarisation

Teaching your puppy to travel in a car is very important if you are going to take him with you anywhere in a car or in other forms of transport. Your breeder may already have accustomed him to travel so that he is relaxed and happy when you collect him and drive him to his new home – if so, this leaves a whole lot less work for you.

Crates are excellent for keeping your puppy safe and secure while travelling. Blankets can be placed in the crate for warmth and comfort and on the sides for extra protection. There are also non-spill water bowls available for travelling. However, if you don't want to use a crate or if there is no room in your car for one, there is also the option of a car harness.

These harnesses usually have a well-padded front and a large loop on the back for the seatbelt to go through. A harness made for walking only is not suitable for using as a car harness and may not give your puppy suitable protection. The car harness allows for a little movement depending on how flexible the seatbelt is. A puppy usually learns quickly to sit or lie down in a car harness safely on the back seat of your car. Your puppy may prefer a car harness or may prefer to travel via crate, you may want to experiment and find out which he prefers.

If you and your puppy prefer the crate option, it is not too hard to get him accustomed to going into a crate in the car. Firstly place the crate on the ground with some blankets, a bowl of water and perhaps a few toys and get your puppy used to having his food in the crate without closing the door. This should take only a couple of days, however, if your puppy takes longer to get used to the crate it's fine, do not rush or push him to go in.

Once the puppy is happy to go into the crate, place the crate into the car and keeping the car door open and the crate open gently lift your puppy into the crate (if you are using a ramp have him walk up the ramp into the car crate). Reward your puppy with treats and sit with him for a few minutes in the car taking care he does not fall or jump out onto the ground. From time to time, close the crate for a few seconds while he is eating or playing with a toy, then open it again so he does not feel he is being trapped.

Next step is to start the engine of the car while your puppy is safely in the crate in the car with his food and toys. Do this for a few minutes a couple of times per day. Make sure the crate door is closed (so he does not jump or fall out) while the engine is running and he is eating or playing with toys. Keep the car static and do not drive anywhere at this stage. Do this a couple of times a day until your puppy is comfortable with the engine running.

The next stage is to drive the car a little distance with your puppy in the car crate. Keep the distance small at first, such as round a block and back home again. Build up the distance a little at a time by about five minutes' drive each day, until your puppy is happy to travel any distance with you. If he begins to get a little car sick, you may be travelling too far, too soon. Reduce the time and build it up again slowly. Not all dogs will enjoy travel but most do learn to be comfortable during travel. Some puppies may learn to sleep through car travel. Providing him with a stuffed kong or other chew type toy may also keep him occupied during long journeys.

Make car travel as comfortable as you can for your puppy and a nice experience. Never leave him alone in a car while you go shopping or leave him alone for any length of time. Puppies may become stressed, worried, anxious, afraid and lonely when left in cars, leading to behaviour problems.

Please remember that dogs and puppies do get hot in cars, which can easily lead to hypothermia, even if you think the weather is not that hot, a car can trap heat and become much hotter than the temperature outside the car. In very cold weather a puppy can also become hypothermic if left freezing. Keep your puppy warm, comfortable, with fresh air, safe and never alone in a car and he should always associate the car and travel as a nice experience.

Is your puppy jumping up on people?

There are three things that puppies find very rewarding from their owners - when you look at them; when you talk to them; or when you touch them. These three rewards should be used for correct behaviour and not for unwanted behaviour.

If your puppy is jumping up on people just ignore the behaviour, fold your arms, say nothing and turn your head and back. This must be done as soon as you anticipate your puppy about to jump up on you. Once the puppy has already jumped up it is a bit late ... try to be ready next time. If you are sitting down when your puppy jumps up on you, turn away in your seat or stand up, say nothing, fold your arms and turn your head and back on the puppy.

You must not look at your puppy, touch your puppy (including pushing him down), or talk to your puppy (including saying "no"). If you look at your dog, push him down, say *no* or shout at him, the behaviour is rewarded and the unwanted jumping up behaviour is increased. Even a negative reward (such as saying *no*) can be seen by your puppy as a positive reward as he is still getting the attention he wants. Therefore he is training you to reward him with attention for his unwanted behaviour.

If you observe other dogs interacting, especially a mother with her puppies, you will see how the mature mother will turn her back or walk away from the younger, immature pups if they get too rough or try to play with her in an unacceptable way. This is not a cruel way of training but a very natural one that dogs themselves use.

For you to be successful in stopping or preventing your puppy jumping up on people, you must be consistent. This is not something that will change overnight - it takes time, consistency and everyone your puppy meets must do the same. You may have to be strong in telling people not to pet your cute puppy for jumping up on them. It is your puppy and you need to protect both him and the people he meets from unwanted behaviour.

If he is getting a reward from time to time from people touching, looking at or speaking to him when he jumps up on them, the unwanted behaviour may increase and become harder to extinguish. Random reward is very strong. You must decide to make sure everyone your puppy meets will not reinforce the unwanted behaviour. The training

71

must be consistent so he gets to know that jumping up on people is never rewarding and the behaviour should eventually stop.

Sometimes a puppy with a strong jumping-up behaviour may become desperate during the training and may start to pull on your clothing or nip your arms when jumping up, in order to get attention. Treat this in the same way, but you can also walk out of the room for a couple of minutes to let the puppy calm down a bit and let him think about what he has done, then walk back in.

You may have to walk out of the room many times, but your consistency will be rewarded in the end. Being consistent is the key to extinguishing this behaviour. Once your puppy is behaving correctly with all four paws on the ground and not jumping up on people you can then reward him with petting and praise.

Another thing that may cause your puppy to jump up is when he is over-excited from too much play, wound up (perhaps fast petting), bored (some dogs don't cope well when humans stop to talk) or stressed, then there is also a greater chance the puppy will jump up.

Keep all petting, movement and praise calm, slow and gentle so as not to wind-up the puppy to jump up again (try not to use a loud, high-pitched voice). Puppies are wound up and stressed by fast movements and high-pitched voices. So keep petting and any movement around your puppy at a slow pace. Watch your puppy's body language and learn from him.

Walking nicely on a slack lead

The first thing I want to ask is: "Why is your puppy pulling?" Perhaps it's because you are following on behind, so it is your puppy who is taking you for the walk rather than vice versa. Therefore your puppy is being rewarded by such a compliant owner who just follows behind and gives a tug of resistance every now and again, which your puppy probably just ignores.

Perhaps he is finding the environment in which you are walking him too much to cope with. If your puppy is getting too excited, aroused or stressed by the environment (look for the calming signals), it may be best to start teaching him in a less stimulating environment so he can learn and cope better.

While your puppy is pulling it may be best to use a harness and a long lead of about two metres or more. The harness will not pulling, but it may protect him from any possible skeletal nerve injury due to pulling on the collar and placing pressure his neck area. If you do not have access to a harness and m a collar, make sure the collar is wide enough to cover at least two vertebrae and is preferably soft and padded.

Start by attaching a long, two-metre lead to your puppy's harness or collar. It is important your puppy is close to you during this technique so you are more likely to have his attention and less likely to go wrong, which is why the puppy is placed on a slack lead rather than off-lead. Keep this lead on all through his training. The lead needs to be long so your dog can still sniff and explore. This sniffing and exploring is not going to be a problem during training and will help your puppy to cope, giving him small breaks when he needs them.

Begin in the least stimulating environment, which may be in your own house or garden. Condition your puppy to a word or sound such as the click sound horse riders use to get a horse to move. It needs to be a sound you use only for this training and not at any other time (do not use a clicker for this exercise).

The sound should not be a word, as we want to avoid the emotion that can go into a word - it's hard to put emotion into a sound (try blowing a kiss when you are angry - it doesn't work!). Condition your puppy by making the sound, then treating your puppy with something nice like a small piece of meat, banana, fruit or vegetable chips, dog biscuit etc, preferably a variety of food that your puppy likes. Repeat a few times.

Take a break for a while. You can then take the next step which is to wait until your puppy is distracted by something (or create a small distraction) then when the puppy's focus has broken from that distraction for a split second, make your sound immediately.

If your timing is right then your puppy should come back to you for a treat. If the timing was wrong, your puppy will probably ignore your sound. Don't worry, just try again the next split second he is distracted. When you are confident your puppy will come directly to you every time you make the noise, even around distractions, then you can take the training to the next level. Never make the sound more than once each time you use it, or your puppy may learn to just ignore the sound. If he does not come after you make the first sound, then practise a little more at getting the timing right.

Start walking very slowly with your puppy on the long lead (allowing full length of the lead to be used by the puppy). Every time you change direction, make your sound as you are about to turn and treat your puppy as he rushes up to get his treat.

Every time your puppy pulls, STOP walking, but do not pull back. Hold the end of the lead into your navel so you have maximum strength to hold your puppy and he should be unable to pull you over. Your navel is your centre of balance and you are less likely to pull your puppy if you already have your hand in tightly to your waist.

Make sure you never tug or pull your puppy. As soon as he starts to look around, make your noise, treat him when he comes to you and carry on walking. Repeat the sound every time you change direction but make sure you don't wear out the sound by making the clicking sound more than once or your puppy may learn to ignore it.

If your puppy ignores you and does not come back to you, ignore him, wait until he turns his head slightly and then make your sound again bringing him back to you, but do not treat him this time since he has ignored you the first time. Your puppy needs to learn he goes nowhere when he pulls, but as soon as he takes the pressure off the

lead, he is allowed to continue to walk. Never get tempt͟ɛ
the lead, leave it the full length for him and he will learn b͟ɪ
will soon become so used to walking with a long lead that ho͟p
you won't want to go back to the short lead again.

When you have mastered this stage, take it to the next level b͟ɪ
making your sound before you are about to turn and just before your
puppy goes right out to the full length of his lead. Just before he gets
to the full length, anticipate him about to pull, make your sound and
have your puppy come back to you and treat him so he learns not
to go too far away and he learns that he is not being rewarded with
a treat for going to the end of the lead or placing pressure on it. This
puts the responsibility upon your puppy to keep the lead slack if he
wishes to continue his walks.

Only give a reward if your puppy responds to your sound the first
time. Once your puppy is walking reasonably well on the loose lead
and responding to your sound each time, you can start to randomly
reward him with treats, instead of every time. This random rewarding
should help to strengthen the behaviour you want because the puppy
never knows when he is getting the treat. You can then begin to
teach this loose lead walking in different environments and then
with different distractions.

The treats can be reduced gradually at a later date when you
have perfected the loose lead walking, but treats should never
stop completely. They are, after all, your dog's reward for correct
behaviour.

This loose lead walking is not an obedience heel. This is for you
and your puppy to have an enjoyable walk together without the
power struggle of pulling going on. If your puppy makes a mistake
or things go wrong do not worry, just come back to the training
again the next day, taking it a few steps back. Better to go back in the
training a few steps so that your puppy has more chance to succeed
and build his confidence again.

Teaching your puppy to *leave it* or *take it*

This task could be life saving to your puppy if he is about to touch
something dangerous or if you break a glass on your kitchen floor
or any other dangerous situation your puppy may find for himself.

You can use the words *leave it* and then take your puppy out of the situation so it can be dealt with while he is out of danger.

You can also use it to prevent your puppy from taking food out of a child's hand and you can also teach your puppy to take treats nicely and many other situations in which this task may be of advantage. However, be careful not to train this exercise near a dog's food bowl as this could create a wrong association and he becomes fearful of eating from his own bowl. Also, some puppies may not like eating from a bowl so you may want to use an extra pair of hands holding treats or another object or toy your puppy likes in order to do this training.

First get your puppy's attention by showing him that you have some very nice food in your left hand (just a little food). When your puppy comes to take the food, close your fist over the food so he can not reach it. Your puppy may try many ways to get the food out of your hand but keep your fist closed and do not allow your puppy to get the food.

Once your puppy realises he is unable to get the food, he may give up for a second or two. This is the time to say *good boy*, open your hand and say *take it* and let him have the food from your right hand.

Repeat this a few times until he learns to pause and wai to open your left hand for him without fighting to get y open.

When he pauses and waits for you to open your hand say *leave u* so he makes the association that not being allowed the food means *leave it*. When you open your hand and allow him to have the food, tell him *take it* and give the food in your right hand so that he makes the association that *take it* means he can have the food.

Remember with all training that puppies have very short concentration levels, so keep all training sessions no more than just a couple of minutes at a time. It may take a few days to teach him this task.

Once your puppy is successfully leaving the treats in your left hand when you ask him, you can then begin to teach him to leave a bowl (or other object) on the floor containing some treats. Do this in the same way you have taught him to leave the treats in your hand. You can use your hand also to cover the bowl, or you can just take it out of his reach when he tries to get to it. Place it back on the ground or uncover it when he leaves it, tell him to *take it* and give him a few treats from your hand, not from the bowl. We are teaching him to leave what could be a dangerous item so we do not want him to dive in and take it after he has left it for a few seconds.

Once your puppy is successfully leaving a plate of treats, you can then teach him to leave other items in the same way, such as a toy on the floor, an item in a person's hand etc. Repeat this task with many different items so your puppy will learn to generalise this task and you can ask him to leave something that could be dangerous to him or possibly something in a child's hand. When you tell him to leave something try to give your puppy something else he can have instead, such as another toy that he is allowed to play with and use your cue word for this, which is *take it*.

Your puppy should learn that the words *leave it* don't always mean he cannot have anything, but rather that he may sometimes get something else equally enjoyable or better. Remember to praise your puppy as much as possible, this will help him make good associations, build his confidence and also help your relationship with him.

Teaching your puppy to *wait*

Your puppy may already be good at waiting without you having to teach it, while some puppies may push past you through doors or jump out of cars before you get a lead on them.

If your puppy is one of those who waits on you going through doors etc, you can still put this behaviour on cue each time he waits by saying the word *wait*, then praise him for waiting. However, if your puppy is one that needs to learn to wait, this is not so hard to teach. Remember to praise him verbally every time he achieves the required behaviour. When you go to the door, begin to open the door just a few centimetres. When your puppy starts to rush to the door in front of you, say nothing (not even no), just block the puppy from going past you by placing your body in the way and close the door. Repeat this until he gets the message and waits. Praise him and take a break. These breaks are important for him as his concentration is short and if you end on a good note, he is more likely to remember the task.

The next stage is to open the door a little further. The puppy may get excited and try again to rush in front of you. Repeat as before, by blocking the doorway with your body and closing the door. Repeat this a few times until the puppy gets the message and waits. Take a break. Repeat this routine opening the door a little more each time until you can open the door wide while he waits.

He does not need to sit, do not try to teach a sit at the same time or you will confuse him. The next stage is for you to go through the door. As you go through, your puppy may try to follow. If this happens say nothing, just repeat as before by blocking the doorway and shutting the door again. Repeat this until the puppy is happy to wait while you go through the door. Once you have him waiting while you go through the door, then add the cue word *wait*. Once you have gone through the door while your puppy waits, you can then tell him to *come* and allow him to come through to you, in which case you can praise him.

You can then repeat this task with other doors he may be rushing through, including your car door. Be careful with car doors – it is so easy to catch his paws, tail or nose in the door. If you repeat this task with many different doors it will help your puppy to generalise so that he is more likely to associate this task with any door he may go through or any situation in which he needs to wait.

You could also take the opportunity to use this task when about

to cross a road or busy street, by telling your puppy to *wait* until you begin to move forward, then tell him to *walk on*. You could ask your puppy to *sit* (providing he has this behaviour on cue) at the curb if you want him to sit while he waits, however, many puppies will not enjoy sitting on wet, rough or prickly ground so be aware of the ground when you ask for a *sit* or a *lie down* at any time.

Chapter seven

Good recall

A good recall is very important for your puppy to learn. If your puppy is in danger, responding to your recall could save his life. When you see other people, dogs or animals ahead, you can call your puppy back to you and go in a different direction or put him back on lead if need be.

To begin teaching your puppy the recall, first choose a word you are going to use as the recall, perhaps the word *come* or *here* or whatever word you want to use. I will use the word *come* for this task.

Choose a large, secure area which could be indoors or out, with no distractions. With the puppy on a harness and long lead, start to amble around the space. As your puppy begins to wander doing his own thing, change direction (remember to walk very slowly) and as the puppy catches up with you, say *good boy* and give a treat instantly. Never lean over your puppy when treating him, make sure you treat him side on, so you are not in a threatening face-on position.

Continue to amble slowly in different directions and as the puppy catches up to you, praise and treat. If the puppy does not catch up to you, say nothing and do not treat, just change direction (never pulling your puppy) and your puppy should soon want to catch up.

If your puppy ignores you crouch down facing away from him. Puppies are curious and will most likely come over to see what's going on. If he comes over when you do this, make sure you do not turn around in his face, but instead allow him to approach you. Tell him *good boy* and reward with a treat. Stand up slowly and walk a little more. Repeat the crouching down if need be.

When your puppy is doing this successfully, unclip the lead and have your puppy repeat the exercise off-lead. We are still not giving the cue word yet, so say nothing else but to praise and treat your puppy.

Once your puppy is doing the exercise off-lead successfully, treat randomly - you may treat the second time he comes to you, then the next time, then the fourth time, then the second again etc. Random reward will help to strengthen the behaviour.

When the puppy is coming to you every time you change direction and staying with you everywhere you amble, put in the cue word *come*, as he comes towards you then praise every time and treat randomly.

Repeat the whole exercise in different places without distraction until he is successful in at least five different places such as your home, a friend's home, a park, a forest, a hall, or any place that he may visit regularly.

Once he is successful in many areas you can then begin to add a few distractions, keeping the distractions at a distance at first and slowly closing the distance making sure he is always successful. He may fail from time to time while learning, but it's okay for him to

do so. Just take a step back and start again. Never tell him off. Just take plenty of breaks and always end on a success if possible. Your puppy can not learn it all in one session, most exercises will take many sessions over many days or even weeks, so be patient and never rush him.

Meeting and greeting

When your puppy greets other puppies such as in puppy classes, or in the forest or park, they will most likely run towards one another and begin to play. This play may go well for a few seconds or a few minutes until one puppy may find it too much and then they start to chase each other or become frantic in their play or perhaps one might try to get behind its owner, a tree or another object as a barrier to protect itself. In most cases puppies do not cope so well with rough-and-tumble after a few minutes or for some just a few seconds.

We need to intervene and help our puppies out by splitting up the unwanted behaviour such as chasing, frantic play, etc, before the puppies become wound up, over excited, worried, insecure or stressed. Many puppies do not cope with this type of full-on meeting and greeting, it depends on the puppy, its temperament and the situation.

There is also risk from the other dog - your puppy's excited greeting behaviour may not be welcomed by some dogs. Some dogs may have been through some nasty experiences with other dogs and may have developed a fear towards other dogs (even pups) that run towards them. If your puppy meets a dog like this and has a nasty experience only once, it could have a devastating effect on how he meets or greets dogs in the future.

Even if both the puppies and owners have good intentions, it is always safest to make sure your puppy is on his lead in a public place where he is likely to meet other dogs, unless you know 100 percent that you can call your puppy back to you well before he can get to the other dog and you can take him in another direction.

It is not always easy to avoid a greeting situation between two dogs - you do not always see what is around the corner or which dogs may be roaming free, off lead.

If this does happen and suddenly a dog is too close and meets your puppy, do not tighten your lead but instead have it completely slack, giving your puppy as much of the lead as possible and keeping it loose. Then try to call him out of the situation by walking off in another direction. If you do not slacken the lead when your puppy meets another dog he may associate the pressure or pain from the tightened lead with the other dog which could lead to fear and other problems with strange dogs.

You may begin to panic a little and start winding up the lead, causing your puppy to feel that he really must have something to worry about with this other dog because he can feel that you are worried. When the puppy starts to worry about greeting other dogs, he may begin to feel so worried that he becomes fearful and needs

After a brief meeting you can split up the puppies by walking between and taking them out of the situation.

to escape. However, on a tight or short lead he is unable to escape. The only way he may be able to express his fear is to bark, growl, or bite the other dog. This may cause problems associated with other dogs to develop. If you want your puppy to become socialised with other dogs, make sure all socialising experiences are pleasant and that your puppy meets mature adult dogs or older puppies correctly.

These are dogs and puppies that will not engage in play, chasing or get wound up when meeting your puppy. They should meet in a calm, relaxed way, curving around each other (not full on directly at one another) and sniffing the anal area before greeting at the head.

The head-on greeting may be achieved with a lot of head turning. If the head turning goes on for more than a few seconds it would help them out a little if you just walk between them and break their focus. They may then just turn around, sniff the ground or walk off.

This behaviour is part of a mature adult greeting. Sometimes, puppies or adult dogs not yet mature may need a little help and intervention from people or mature dogs. If you plan to take regular social walks with your puppy and another dog the puppy has not yet met, it may be best to allow them to meet at a distance first.

The reason for this is to allow your puppy and the other dog to choose if they want to meet, if they can walk nicely together and to prevent full-on rushing at one another.

This greeting can be done by a technique called parallel walking.

Parallel walking

Have the dogs on long slack leads with their owners at the same end of a large field but a good distance between them, say about 30 metres (depending on how much space the dogs need), and begin walking, keeping at the same parallel distance.

Begin walking very slowly. If one dog stops to sniff, the other stops to keep parallel. Try to stay in a straight line so that you do not drift any closer to one another. Continue this walking up and down the field a few times. If the dogs are coping well and not worried about each other, then move a few metres closer.

During parallel walking trees, humans or other objects can be used as barriers to help the dogs cope.

Go up and down the field again a few times, and then take a break for at least an hour, letting your puppy rest during this break, or come back another day for the next step.

The next session can start as for the first session but just walk up and down the field once, then move in a little closer and walk up and down a couple of times. If your puppy is not coping, go back to making more space between the two dogs, walk up and down a couple more times and take a break.

When your puppy is coping well with the distance, then you can move a little closer. Gradually move in closer and closer, but not too quickly and keeping a close eye on your puppy's calming signals. If he starts to get a little worried, i.e. lungeing, barking, lip licking, head dipping, hiding behind you, then make more distance between them again, giving them more time and space to become familiar with one another.

When the dogs are getting close enough so that there is only a few metres between them, take them out of the situation and take a break. Do not force a meeting.

During this next session your puppy and the other dog may or may not wish to meet. Respect what your puppy wants and do not push the issue. The focus should not be to make the dogs meet. This choice should be given to the dogs. The parallel walking is to find out if the dogs want to walk together.

Start your parallel walking again at a good distance and slowly move in as you walk up and down the field parallel to one another. When you are just a few metres from one another and your puppy and other dog wish to meet (look at the calming signals) you can allow them a very brief meeting, keeping the leads slack, and then call them out of the situation. Take a break.

During the next session the dogs can begin the parallel walking at a close distance so they can meet if they wish but do not push them to meet. Walk up and down the field side by side on a slack lead giving them the opportunity to make their own choices whether or not they wish to greet each other or just walk, sniff and explore the environment. If they are happy to walk calmly with one another, explore and sniff, they will most likely get on fine and should enjoy walking together regularly.

If your puppy or both dogs are barking, lungeing, jumping on one another, using barriers to get away, cowering etc, then it's too soon for them to meet. Go back to the beginning and stay there for a few weeks until they are ready to move closer again or use a calmer, more mature dog to walk with your puppy.

Preparing your puppy for a new baby

When puppy and baby are introduced correctly, the experience can be safe and pleasant for your puppy, baby and family members. Not all puppies like babies. However, this does not mean they cannot live in harmony with one another.

Before the new baby is born, it may be wise to begin introducing the puppy to baby items and smells, allowing him to be part of the preparations. Let him sniff in the baby's room at all the baby bedding, clothing, pushchair, toiletries and toys etc. This allows him to get used to this room being occupied and the new smells that go with it.

Puppies can get upset or frustrated when there is change in the household, a change in the amount of attention they usually receive from their owner, or a change to the routine. These changes can cause a degree of stress in your puppy's behaviour as he may find

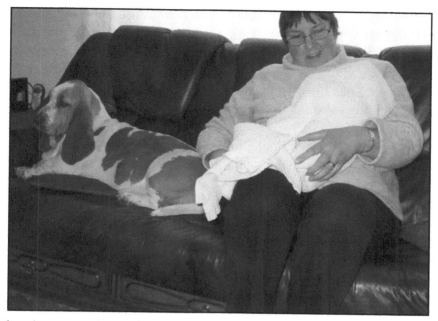

the changes a little difficult to cope with.

Even if you are the most calm and relaxed person around your puppy, there will be times of tension. Be patient as he is trying to make a big adjustment, just as his humans are.

Try to get into a routine of how life will be when the baby is around. Try using a large baby doll and carry it around. Put the doll in a high chair at times, put the doll in the push chair from time to time and push it around the house. Sit with your puppy, having the doll on one arm while massaging or gently stroking and talking to your puppy nicely.

You may feel a bit silly carrying a doll around but the more you do this and treat it as if it's a real baby, it may be easier for your puppy to accept what's going on and he is more likely to learn how to react towards the real baby when it arrives. Remember to praise your puppy for all good behaviour towards the doll.

Turn on the baby's lullaby tunes and toys from time to time (don't overdo the sounds) so the puppy gets used to these sounds. There are also CDs available with the sounds of babies crying on them. These CDs can be played at a low level for about two minutes a couple of times a day so your puppy gets used to the sound of a baby. There are usually instructions with these CDs on how to use the programmes.

Purchase a few new toys for your puppy just before the baby arrives and make sure he has a place such as a bed, open crate or blankets, to which he can go and get out of the way if he chooses. This way he has his own space, his own toys and a place to escape to and de-stress should all the new baby sounds and activity get a bit much for him.

When baby comes home, allow the puppy to safely sniff the baby (not the baby's face) if he wants to (as long as it is safe to do so) while the baby is in your protective arms. The puppy will be curious and need to see and sniff the baby. Some puppies will love having a new baby around and others will just sniff and turn their backs as if to say "thanks but no thanks, not for me". This is okay and it is the puppy's own choice to like or dislike babies. You cannot make him like a baby if he doesn't want to. This need not be a problem and does not necessarily mean he will growl at or harm the baby in any way.

It is up to us to respect the puppy's choice and manage the situation by helping him out and giving him space when the baby is around. Make sure his bedding, especially at night, is as far away from the baby's room as possible so that the puppy gets the least disturbance and disruption to his routine as possible if the baby wakes in the night.

When nursing the baby during the day, make sure the puppy also has something of his own to chew. Perhaps give him his dinners when baby has her dinners or give him a food-stuffed kong, treat ball or some type of quality chew treat your puppy likes so that he feels a sense of belonging, not one of being left out when you are busy with the baby.

If the puppy really loves the baby and will continue to go into the baby's bedroom to wake it up, put a dog gate in the doorway of the baby's room to prevent him from going in there. Never leave your puppy alone with a baby or child without supervision.

If you have taught your puppy the words *leave it* they could be very handy words in stopping your puppy going into the baby's room or approaching the baby on the floor. However, baby-dog gates are very helpful and prevention is always better than having to use a lot of commands. Never shout at your puppy, strike him or say *no* or do anything that would cause your puppy any pain or fear in front of the baby. Dogs learn by association and if he is looking at your baby at the time he experiences the pain, or negative experience, he may associate it with the baby and begin to fear babies which may lead to behaviour problems with babies and small children.

As your baby grows he or she may begin to show interest in the puppy. If your puppy is not used to being touched on different parts of his body it may be worthwhile getting him used to being touched before the baby begins touching and perhaps grabbing or pulling him from time to time. You can do this during your puppy's daily massage times for a few minutes each day. When stroking or massaging your puppy be sure to stroke his ears, nose, tail, and as many parts of his body that he will allow you to touch. Build this up slowly so he will comfortably allow you to hold his ear or tail for one or two seconds, then he should cope better when the baby touches him.

Make sure every experience your puppy has around your baby or any other babies or children is pleasant, then puppy, baby and family will have a better opportunity to live in harmony with one another.

Introducing a puppy to an elderly dog

If you already have an elderly dog in your household you will need to introduce your puppy to him correctly so it is done in a stress-free way, giving them an enjoyable experience of one another and to give them the time and space they need, away from one another.

When the new puppy arrives home, it may be best to keep him away from the older dog at first, until he has explored the house inside and out. The puppy and older dog will be aware of one another's smell.

If possible try to have them meet in neutral territory, doing a little parallel walking as explained earlier in this chapter, closing the distance slowly until they meet. If the meeting goes well they should be okay when they meet each other in the home.

If it is not possible for them to meet in neutral territory then using a stair-dog gate (puppy play pen can also be used) allows your older dog and puppy to see each other through the gate. At this stage we do not want them to meet but just to view each other through the gate. They may show signs of wanting to meet and the puppy may even bark.

If your puppy barks at your older dog just go between, blocking your puppy's view with your body and have someone distract the puppy with something while you take your older dog away from the puppy's view. From time to time (once every couple of hours when puppy is awake) allow them to see each other through the gate.

If puppy begins to bark, again block his view with your body while someone distracts him and take the older dog out of view. Do this until the puppy can calmly accept the older dog or vice-versa if the older dog is the one barking. Once they can accept one another's presence then they can be left in view for a few minutes at a time.

It may be the next day before they can greet each other, or a few days depending on the dogs, but this is okay, they do not need to meet each other on the first day if they are not ready. When the time comes for them to meet, try to make the greeting outdoors if possible in a safe place or indoors with escape routes for both of them, should one feel the need to get out of the situation.

There are a few ways in which you can help make the greeting a little easier for them. You can provide an enriched environment to give them both other things to sniff and focus on if one or both are feeling a little worried about the greeting.

This elderly dog is protected behind the dog gate.

You can also be there close-by, to go between and split up if the puppy is a bit much for the older dog. It may be easier to place the puppy or both on a harness and long lead when the first greeting is done, provided the puppy has been used to a harness and lead. Make sure they have a slack lead as they meet each other or any people, and you need to be ready to split up and go between to help them out. Your older dog needs to know he is still safe and protected by you. He needs to know you are there to help him out when he is not coping with the puppy and that you will take him out of the situation when he needs an escape.

No dog, especially an elderly dog, should be made to put up with the rough-and-tumble of an active or boisterous puppy.

Dog stair gates are excellent tools for helping out elderly dogs or any other dogs you may have in the house. This will help give the dogs and the puppy the space and time out they need and a safe place to escape to and be on their own when need be.

An elderly or adolescent dog can also be far too active for a puppy. Any rushing at one another, body slamming, or rough-and-tumble with a small puppy can cause the puppy serious injury. Many puppies have been seriously injured by older dogs when play gets too rough.

Always watch for those calming signals and help them out making use of the gates, play pens or other barriers to protect your elderly dog and your new puppy.

Do your best to follow these routines and you should have many happy years together with your new puppy.

Recommended reading, viewing or research

Calming signals – What your dog tells you (DVD) – Turid Rugaas
Understanding & training your puppy (DVD) – Nina Bondarenko

On talking terms with dogs (calming signals) – Turid Rugaas
What do I do when my dog pulls – Turid Rugaas
Kingdom of the senses - Anne-Lill Kvam
Your dogs senses – Brigitte Rauth-Widmann
Playtime for your dog - Christina Sandermann
Natural health for dogs & cats - Richard H Pitcairn
Herbal dog care – Randy Kidd
Wild health – Cindy Engel
When elephants weep – J Masson & S McCarthy
Dog homoeopathic remedies - George McLeod
Why zebras don't get ulcers – Robert M Sapolsky
The ageing dog – Carl Gorman
The behavioural effects of canine castration - Hazel Palmer
Dog friendly gardens, garden friendly dogs - Cheryl Smith
Dog anatomy - Peter Goody
Will my pet go to heaven – Steve Wholeberg
Bones would rain from the sky – Suzanne Clothier
The other end of the leash – Patricia McConnell
The culture clash – Jean Donaldson
Don't shoot the dog – Karen Pryor
Dominance fact or fiction – Barry Eaton
Dogwatch - Desmond Morris

Shalva Canine Centre – www.shalvaholistics.com
K9 Perspective magazine - www.k9magazinefree.com
Pet Dog Trainers of Europe - www.pet-dog-trainers-europe.com
Sheila Harper Canine Education – www.sheilaharper.co.uk
Dog Training International - www.turid-rugaas.no
Canine Bowen Technique – www.caninebowentechnique.com
European animal trainer - www.animaltrainer.eu
Troll dog school Norway - www.troll-hundeskole.com

Bible Quote: Proverbs 12v10: A righteous man cares for the needs of his animals.

Notes:

Observations:

Veterinary and health record:

L - #0498 - 060420 - C0 - 229/152/6 - PB - DID2808293